Reader's Digest

Fruit & Vegetable Gardening

Published by
The Reader's Digest Association Limited
London • New York • Sydney • Montreal

contents

The vegetable garden

The fruit garden

the
vegetable
garden

8 Garden basics

BEFORE YOU START TO PLANT VEGETABLES OR FRUIT IN YOUR GARDEN, YOU NEED TO MAKE SURE THAT THE SOIL THAT YOU ARE PLANTING INTO IS IN GOOD ENOUGH SHAPE TO ALLOW YOUR CROPS THE BEST POSSIBLE START. LEARNING YOUR SOIL TYPE, THEN ADDING THE CORRECT KIND OF NUTRIENTS AND DIGGING OVER ARE ESSENTIAL FOR A SUCCESSFUL CROP.

Preparing the soil

Identifying the soil in your garden
Knowledge of soil type is an essential aid to successful planting. Take note of the plants growing naturally in your neighbourhood to help you to determine the soil type. An acid soil is indicated by the presence of broom, foxgloves, gorse, heaths and heathers, Scots and maritime pines and speedwell. Cranesbill, various field poppies, juniper, thistles and wild cherry trees grow in alkaline soil.

Testing the pH of your soil It is easy to determine the pH level of your soil using a simple test kit from a garden centre. Usually, a tablet is added to a soil sample dissolved in water. Any colour change in the solution is compared with colours on a test card to give the pH level on a scale of 1 to 14; below 7 is acid and above 7 is alkaline.

Improving the structure of soil Adding organic matter can improve the texture of both heavy and light soils. Clay soil becomes easier to dig and soil particles stick together so drainage is improved. In sandy soils it soaks up moisture that is then more available to plants.

Testing soil in the hand

Do a simple hand test to help to determine the soil type in your garden. Lift up and rub a ball of moist soil between your fingers. It may be necessary to moisten the soil but do not get it too wet.

- **Sand** If the soil breaks up and feels gritty it contains sand; largish particles signal grit. Sandy soil warms quickly in spring, is light and easy to manage and is rarely waterlogged. It does require constant feeding and watering because water and nutrients drain through so quickly.
- **Clay** If the soil smears smoothly and appears slightly shiny it contains a lot of clay. A heavy clay soil stays cold and is difficult to dig. It can become waterlogged in wet weather yet bakes hard in drought. It contains plenty of nutrients.
- **Silt** If the soil feels soapy and sticky it is a silt.
- **Loam** If the soil starts to smear then breaks up, it is probably a loam, which has been improved over the years and will allow a very wide range of garden plants to be grown.

Sources of organic matter

- **Compost** See opposite for making compost
- **Leaf mould** A good way to compost leaves is to fill several plastic sacks with leaves and some garden soil. When the sack is full, tie the neck and punch a few holes in the side. Leave the bags for at least six months until the leaves have rotted to a dark brown, crumbly texture (see box on page 10).
- **Manure** Animal manure has plenty of useful nutrients and benefits the structure of the soil. Always use well-rotted manure. Horse manure rots more quickly than that from cows and pigs and is readily available. Either stack it in a pile to rot down or add to the compost heap.

Other sources of organic matter

- **Mushroom compost** – rotted horse manure previously used for growing mushrooms. It is not suitable for alkaline soils.
- **Spent hops** – available from breweries – they can be difficult to handle because they are wet.
- **Seaweed** – rich in nutrients but wet and bulky so should be used sparingly.

Compost

There are two different kinds of compost: Garden compost is made by rotting down vegetable matter and is used to improve the soil. It should not be used for sowing seeds or potting plants. Seed and potting composts are special formulations, often based on peat, coir or loam, specifically for sowing seeds or potting plants.

Chose the site for your compost heaps carefully. You need a corner of the garden that has easy access for a wheelbarrow and is generally hidden from view.

Ready-made bins You can buy plastic compost bins suitable for a small garden. They have ventilated walls, a lift-up panel and a weatherproof top and will produce usable compost in three to four months in summer and six to eight months in winter.

Making your own bins If you have space, it is best to have a pair of compost bins so that the contents of one can be left to mature while the other is being filled. Bins of 1 m^3 should supply enough compost for an average garden. You can build your own bins. Start with six 1.2m fence posts treated with a solvent-based wood preservative. Drive them into the ground 1m apart to a depth of 30cm. Using galvanised nails attach planks across the back, sides and centre of the structure. The plants can be old floorboards, scaffolding planks or strips from wooden pallets. Paint the boards with preservative.

Compost making Start off your compost heap with a 25cm layer of garden waste. Water if dry and cover with a 5cm layer of soil. Build up the heap with similar layers until it reaches the top of the bin, sprinkling one layer with a compost activator and the next with 138g per m^2 of garden lime. Cover the top with a lid or old carpet to keep in the heat.

What to compost? Lawn mowings, vegetable peelings and dust from a vacuum cleaner bag if you have woollen carpets, break down quickly. Hedge clippings and tree prunings are best shredded before being added. Bulky waste such as cabbage leaves and shreddy woody stems should be mixed with fine material such as lawn mowings, before adding to the heap. Leaves should be stored separately in an uncovered mesh container and to turn into leaf mould.

Aerate the heap When the compost heap is completed, plunge an old broom handle or metal rod into it to make vertical holes for aeration. Make sure the rod is long enough to penetrate the heap from top to bottom.

Adding organic matter

1 You can use fresh organic matter if you spread it on a clear vegetable plot in autumn. It will rot in time before you sow and plant in spring.

2 Place it at the bottom of a trench and cover it with soil – a good method for thirsty, deep-rooted plants.

3 Mix it into the soil with a fork or spade.

Some plants are grown to be dug into the soil – the most popular are pulses and alfalfa, clover, agricultural lupin, vetch and

The front of the compost bin should be made of wooden bars or palings that can be lifted out so that you can get to the compost.

other plants with nitrogen fixing properties. Sow in late summer and early autumn and cut down in spring. Dig the plants in while they are young to prevent them from self-seeding and spreading.

Digging

How often should you dig? Digging breaks up and aerates the soil, it buries the weeds and exposes soil pests to be eaten by the birds or killed by frost. However, digging too often can upset the ecological balance of the soil by interfering with micro-organism activity, which helps to break down organic matter and aids the absorption of nutrients by plant roots. Thorough digging once a year is generally all that is needed.

The best time to dig Ideally, dig in autumn to bury old weed growth, incorporate organic material and expose the clods of soil to frost, which will break them up. If a green manure crop is to be grown over winter, dig the soil during late summer and sow the crop immediately.

■ Avoid digging when the soil is too wet, which can damage its structure and cause it to compact. Squeeze a handful of the soil. If it crumbles it is all right to dig, but if it sticks together it is too wet.

Digging techniques Simple digging – lifting out a spade's depth of soil and turning it over – is adequate when working on cultivated beds, but if you are preparing a new bed or digging in a lot of organic matter, single or double digging is preferable. These techniques involve digging a series of trenches to a single or double spade's depth, and filling each empty trench with soil from the next as you dig. This increases the depth of the topsoil, breaks up compacted soil and improves drainage.

■ On shallow soils, dig down to the subsoil and incorporate small amounts of topsoil into the subsoil to increase the depth of cultivated ground.

Watch your back Do not overreach yourself by tackling too large an area or by attempting to take up too much earth with each spadeful – you should be able to lift it

Making leaf mould

1 Rake up autumn leaves, preferably after rain. Stack them outdoors in a simple low enclosure. Tread down the leaves to make room for more. Leave the heap open, or cover with old carpet or sacking.

2 The level of leaf-mould will fall as the leaves decay, and you can sometimes combine two heaps into one after a year. By this time, the partially decomposed leaf-mould makes an excellent soil conditioner and mulch.

3 If you allow leaf-mould to rot for two years, you can sieve out the finer material and add it to potting composts and top-dressings for lawns.

Apply organic matter as a surface layer or mulch which will then be carried down into the soil by earthworms.

without difficulty. Bend knees and elbows rather than your back while lifting the spade. Spread out the work – two hours a day, or digging about 20m² of soil that is neither too heavy nor too stony, is enough. Any more and you will wear yourself out.

Spring digging and weed control Digging in spring can bring thousands of weed seeds to the surface, which will then germinate.

- Hold off sowing until the weeds have grown and you have cleared them to produce a clean seedbed for your crops and flowers. If the soil is dry, watering stimulates weed growth and speeds up the process.

The no-digging method When conditions are dry, digging on a light soil can cause valuable moisture to be lost. An alternative is to cover the soil with a thick layer of well-rotted compost or manure. This layer protects the soil from water loss and compaction, and is gradually drawn into the soil by worms. Their busy activity helps drainage and aeration.

Getting ready to plant

Controlling weeds Bare, weed-free soil is much easier to cultivate than ground covered with growth. Weeds will take nutrients out of the soil, encourage pests and diseases and make the garden look untidy.

- Keep freshly cultivated soil clear of weeds by covering the area with old carpet. Leave it in place until you are ready to use the ground. On small areas, recycle flattened cardboard boxes covered with a layer of soil. The cardboard controls the weeds and rots to add organic matter to the soil.
- If weeds have developed in the plot where you are intending to plant, mow them down right after they flower. If you let them go to seed, you will have to contend with generations of hardy survivors.

Before you sow or plant Dig only well-rotted compost and manure into the soil. Fresh material should be left in a heap to decompose before it is dug in, while partially broken-down material can be spread over the soil surface as a mulch that will gradually rot and be taken into the soil by worm activity.

- You can enrich a mulch with wood ash, poultry manure, phosphate-rich bone meal, nitrogen-rich dried blood, or blood, fish and bone meal, a balanced general feed. You can also use nettle manure to improve the soil.

Rake over the soil Before sowing seeds or planting out small seedlings, it is important to break up the soil surface into a fine crumbly texture so that plant roots will establish quickly. Rake over the surface with a soil rake until large clods are broken down to a fine, level finish – called a fine 'tilth'. Remove large stones and remaining weeds.

- **The best way to rake** Hold the rake like a broom, as upright as possible. The teeth should be almost parallel to the soil, so they do not go too deep. Work evenly back and forth in small sections.

Hoe lightly Avoid hoeing more than 5cm deep. This shallow action will cut off new weed growth near the soil surface but at the same time avoid bringing up more seeds from lower down. Weed seeds buried below 5cm are unlikely to germinate and grow.

- Keep a hoe to hand, ready to take with you whenever you walk around your garden, so you can 'worry away at the weeds' and it doesn't become a large-scale job.

12 Creating a vegetable plot

IT IS POSSIBLE TO INCLUDE A FEW FAVOURITE VEGETABLES ALMOST ANYWHERE IN THE GARDEN, BUT THE TIME MAY COME WHEN YOU WANT TO GROW A MORE AMBITIOUS SELECTION OF CROPS IN A DEDICATED KITCHEN GARDEN OR VEGETABLE PLOT. AT THIS STAGE, SOME THOUGHT AND PLANNING WILL PAY DIVIDENDS.

With careful planning, you can grow a variety of different vegetables even in a relatively small urban garden.

The right site

Choosing the best place to grow vegetables is important, as it can make the difference between success and failure. Factors to consider include:

■ **Shelter** Cold winds seriously affect cropping, with even light winds reducing yields by 20 per cent or more, especially in winter. Fences and hedges filter winds and limit their impact, and both can be used to protect vegetables and fruit crops, adding to the total productivity of your garden. Walls can be a mixed blessing. They are valuable for supporting trained fruit, but solid barriers can produce strong wind turbulence within the garden and trap frost. Make sure that boundary or internal walls are not affecting the proposed site adversely.

■ **Sun and shade** Most crops need plenty of sunlight, particularly winter crops, if they are to yield well. Light shade can be welcome in summer to protect leafy vegetables like lettuce and kohlrabi from drying out, but heavy shade from buildings or trees is best avoided.

■ **Good drainage** Heavy waterlogged soil causes all kinds of problems for vegetables. If puddles tend to lie on the surface for any length of time after prolonged rain, you might have to dig the site deeply to improve drainage, or consider raising the soil level in beds or ridges to increase the depth of well-drained earth.

■ **Soil** No soil is perfect, but most can be improved over time. Incorporating large amounts of organic material, such as garden compost and rotted manure, adds body to light soils and opens up heavy clays. With regular cultivating and mulching, your soil and crops will steadily improve in quality.

■ **Size** Even a small area can be productive, but plot size will affect the choice of plants you will be able grow. If you have a small plot, choose vegetables that can grow close together. Include tall plants that use vertical space, like beans, and crop the ground intensively by spacing the plants closely.

A practical design

In drawing up a plan for your vegetable plot, try to incorporate the permanent features listed right. Some of these will make your day-to-day gardening easier, while others, like paths, form a key part of the layout.

Permanent features

■ **Compost bins** allow you to dispose of annual weeds and vegetable waste, and to recycle their fertility back into the garden.
■ **Space** to stack manure, leaf-mould and other bulky materials for digging into and improving the soil.
■ **Water** – you don't want to carry this far, so consider installing a tap and standpipe, or a tank to collect rainwater.
■ **A coldframe**
■ **Borders or other space** for herbs and perennial vegetables, such as asparagus and globe artichokes.

Making a traditional vegetable plot

You need • spade • rake • string • pegs • measuring tape • 16 treated timber boards 8–10cm wide by 2.5cm thick • 16 30cm battens • sledgehammer • screwdriver • screws • cocoa shells and grit, or bark

1 Dig the site, removing weeds, especially the roots of perennial species. Rake the area level.

2 Using string and pegs, mark out a square. Divide into quarters with two central paths 50cm wide, crossing at right angles.

3 Edge beds with the treated boards. Drive battens firmly into the ground at the corners of the beds and screw boards to these.

4 Surface paths with a layer of cocoa shells and grit or shredded bark. For a permanent surface, such as brick, dig out some soil and spread it on the beds before laying the paving material.

5 Number beds for crop rotation. Bed 1 Add rotted manure for peas and beans. 2 Add garden compost and fertiliser for potatoes. 3 Add fertiliser for root crops. 4 Compost and fertiliser for brassicas.

6 Rake the beds level, and plant any edging crops of perennial herbs, flowers or low hedges. Water in well. You are now ready to plan plantings for each bed.

Mixed cropping in the vegetable garden

Some gardeners believe that certain vegetables grow better in association with particular neighbours. Here are some traditional 'friends and foes' for mixed or companion planting schemes.

PLANT	GOOD COMPANIONS	BAD COMPANIONS
ASPARAGUS	Leeks, parsley, peas, tomatoes	Beetroot
BEETROOT	Cabbage, celery, green beans, lettuce, onion	Asparagus, tomatoes
BROAD BEANS	Lettuce, parsnips, potatoes	
CABBAGE	Beetroot, celery, cucumber, green beans, lettuce, parsnips, peas, potatoes, tomatoes	Onions, radishes
CARROTS	Green beans, leeks, lettuce, onions, parsnips, peas, radishes	
CELERY	Beetroot, cabbage, cucumber, fennel, green beans, leeks, peas, potatoes, tomatoes	
COURGETTES	Green beans, potatoes, sweetcorn	Cabbage, fennel
CUCUMBER	Cabbage, celery, green beans, lettuce, peas, sweetcorn	Potatoes, tomatoes
FENNEL	Celery, leeks	Cabbage, green beans, tomatoes
GREEN BEANS	Cabbage, carrots, celery, courgettes, cucumber, leeks, lettuce, marrows, peas, potatoes, radishes, sweetcorn, tomatoes	Beetroot, fennel, onions
LEEKS	Asparagus, carrots, celery, fennel, lettuce, onions, tomatoes	Beetroot, cabbage
LETTUCE	Beetroot, broad beans, cabbage, carrots, cucumber, green beans, leeks, onions, peas, radishes, turnips	Parsley
MARROWS	Green beans, potatoes, sweetcorn	Cabbage, fennel
ONIONS	Beetroot, carrots, leeks, lettuce, parsnips, tomatoes	Cabbage, green beans, peas, potatoes
PARSLEY	Asparagus, tomatoes	Celery, lettuce, peas
PARSNIPS	Broad beans, cabbage, carrots, onions	
PEAS	Asparagus, cabbage, carrots, celery, cucumber, green beans, lettuce, sweetcorn, turnips, potatoes, radishes	Garlic, onions, parsley
POTATOES	Broad beans, cabbage, celery, green beans, peas, tomatoes	Courgettes, cucumber, onions, sweetcorn
RADISHES	Broad beans, carrots, cucumbers, green beans, lettuce, parsley, peas, spinach, tomatoes	Cabbage
SPINACH	Most vegetables	
SWEETCORN	Courgettes, cucumber, green beans, marrows, peas	Potatoes
TOMATOES	Asparagus, cabbage, celery, green beans, leeks, onions, parsley, potatoes, radishes	Beetroot, cucumber, fennel
TURNIPS	Lettuce, peas	

■ **Fruits** – both trees and soft fruits – are permanent and should be considered early in the planning stage.
■ **Paths** provide essential access, both for cultivation and for harvesting, particularly on a wet day. Depending on the size of your plot, you will need at least one all-weather path, ideally wide enough to manoeuvre a wheelbarrow. Narrower paths between beds can be of beaten earth or made from more durable materials.
■ **Edges to beds** such as treated timber boards, bricks or a low hedge of perennial herbs, keep the paths clean.

Crop rotation

Growing vegetables in a new position each year is an important precaution against building up soil pests and diseases, and depleting soil nutrients. The traditional method is to divide the ground into three or four plots or beds, then move groups of vegetables with similar needs and disorders from one bed to the next in annual sequence. The three main groups are legumes (peas and beans), brassicas (the cabbage family), and root crops, including onions, with potatoes and squashes in a fourth bed. Fit in salad leaves and sweetcorn wherever there is space. Additions of rotted manure or garden compost are made to each bed when digging and preparing it for planting, depending on the type of crop grown in it (see page 13). Fertiliser, where required, is applied just before planting the crop. In small gardens, where only a few vegetables are grown, simply avoid growing a particular group or individual crop in the same place for two consecutive years.

Style and layout

There are a number of alternative layouts to the traditional one shown in the box on page 13, which also make efficient use of the space. And a vegetable garden need not always be strictly functional, as many crops are ornamental as well as edible.

■ **Traditional kitchen gardens** were quartered by crossing paths, a system that allowed for efficient crop rotation and a large number of bed edges that could be planted with herbs, soft fruits or flowers for cutting.
■ **Raised or narrow beds,** up to 1.2m wide, are very productive; they make the most of small spaces and organic matter and are useful in planning crop rotations too. Several can be arranged to form a kitchen garden, or you can include them as an integral part of a flower border.
■ **Potagers** are plots that exploit the decorative potential of vegetables by arranging them like bedding plants, balancing their shapes and colours in a pattern of formally shaped beds.
■ **A cottage garden patchwork** can be made by organising small square beds in a flexible layout for any size or shape of site, perhaps combined with flowers.

No-dig beds

The deep bed, or no-dig, system of cultivation is based on the concept that routine cultivation damages the soil structure and can lead to a reduction in the population of worms and other beneficial organisms within the soil.

Instead of digging the soil to work in organic matter, the organic matter is spread over the surface and left for worms and other organisms to gradually draw it down into the upper layers, improving fertility in the area penetrated by most plant roots. Worm activity not only breaks down organic matter but improves the soil's aeration, drainage and water-holding capacity.

The no-dig system is particularly suitable for dealing with heavy clay soils, which are difficult to work and are easily compacted. By protecting the surface with organic matter, structural damage is avoided, while below the surface worms can open up the soil's close structure and help to improve its drainage.

Maintaining a no-dig bed

1 Mulch the surface every year with well-rotted organic matter to a depth of about 10cm to keep soil fertile. This deep mulching will reduce moisture loss, suppress the germination of weed seeds and keep the soil warmer, extending the growing season. Always work from a path.

2 When you want to plant, scrape back the mulch to expose the soil surface and replace it afterwards, keeping it clear of young stems. The timber edging helps to retain the mulch layer within the bed until it rots down.

Preparation

A once-only, very thorough cultivation is essential to the success of the no-dig system. Double digging, incorporating large quantities of organic matter, enriches the soil and improves texture. But from this point on, any cultivation and walking on beds must be avoided to prevent disturbance or compaction, and to allow a natural soil structure to develop. For this reason you need to be able to reach to the middle of the bed comfortably from either side, which limits the width to about 1.2m.

Choosing your crops

To some extent, deciding what to grow is a matter of trial and error, but it is a good idea to start with vegetables that are favourites with your family and also those that are expensive, or hard to find, in the shops.

- **List your favourite vegetables** and decide what not to grow. Good-quality maincrop potatoes and cabbages may be available locally, whereas salad leaves, sweetcorn or early baby carrots taste better picked fresh.
- **Match your list to the available space**, and the time and energy you can devote to their cultivation. Recognise the difference between vegetables that sprint to maturity, allowing you to grow something else afterwards, and slow crops such as Brussels sprouts that need a long growing season.
- **Use your space to best effect**. Do you want to harvest a wide variety of produce for as long as possible, or simply raise large amounts of a few varieties for storing or self-indulgence?
- **Find out what does well locally** As your soil and skills improve, your range of produce will increase, but some crops may not suit your soil or climate.
- **Keep a garden diary**. Note your most successful crops and varieties, with their sowing or planting dates, to help you to plan for the next year.

Raising from seed

The cheapest and possibly the most rewarding way to grow vegetables is to raise them from seed, but this depends on having a greenhouse or at least a coldframe to start plants off in the warmth. Growing from seed gives you a wider choice of vegetables and allows you to select more unusual varieties.

Buying plug plants

Where space is at a premium, it is a good idea to buy plug plants or small trays of seedlings. You can buy only as many plants as you have space to grow. You can buy a wide range of crops in this form, both from garden centres and through mail-order and internet outlets.

Plug plants and seedlings are also an invaluable way of raising vegetables if you do not have a greenhouse or a coldframe, and prefer not to propagate on windowsills. Let the professionals germinate the seeds and grow on the young plants in controlled conditions. You can take over in spring, when growing conditions are better.

Cropping continuity

The challenge of vegetable growing is keeping a range of crops all year. There are various ways in which you can make the most of your plot and keep it healthy.

- **Successional sowing** It is usually quick-maturing crops like spinach, beetroot, radishes and lettuce that tend to produce gluts and gaps. You can avoided this if you sow small amounts of seed at regular intervals. A good guide is to sow a new batch of seed when the first true leaves (those forming after the seed leaves) start to emerge on the previous sowing. In this way you should be able to avoid 'bolting' lettuces, woody roots or bitter spinach leaves.
- **Intercropping** This means using the space between slow-growing crops as a seedbed for vegetables that are quick to mature or will need transplanting. Radishes, rocket, lettuce, turnips and young beetroot are suitable for growing between winter cabbages, Brussels sprouts or parsnips, spaced a little farther apart than usual.
- **Catch crops** Take advantage of vacant soil by growing a 'catch', or quick-maturing, crop. Rapidly maturing lettuce, spinach or peas could precede a tender crop of runner beans, tomatoes, sweetcorn or courgettes, which can't be planted until the frosts are over. The catch crop is harvested before the tender crop is planted, or gets established.

Maximising your space

Make full use of available ground by spacing plants equally in each direction rather than in rows. This planting 'on the square' (or in staggered rows) works well in a bed system, where equally spaced plants grow evenly and weeds are quickly crowded out. Spacing plants closer than recommended produces 'baby' vegetables, especially with root crops.

Small gardens

If you have a really tiny garden that cannot accommodate dedicated vegetable beds, you can still grow a few vegetables.

- **Flower borders** A number of vegetables have handsome foliage, which looks good among the flowers. Chard has yellow, orange, pink and ruby red stems. Carrot foliage is soft and ferny, and spinach beet and frilly loose-leaved lettuces can be grown as cut-and-come-again crops. Sweetcorn can be planted in a group in a sunny spot. Runner or climbing French beans can be trained up vertical canes at the back of a border, or along a boundary.
- **Containers** Tomatoes and salad crops, peas, beans, courgettes and squash are easy to grow in containers. Early potatoes can be grown in a deep container. Fill it a third full of soil-based compost, space out sprouted seed tubers and cover with more compost. As the foliage appears, fill with compost until the container is full. To harvest, scrape away compost and lift a helping at a time. Cover up the remaining potatoes to grow on.
- **Window boxes** Choose shallow-rooted crops, although carrots with ball-like roots and radishes should also succeed. Peppers and cherry tomatoes crop well in a sunny aspect, if well fed and watered. Bush tomato varieties like 'Tumbler' will even grow successfully in a hanging basket. Lettuces and salad leaves do best on a windowsill shaded from the midday sun.

18 Leafy green vegetables

CABBAGES AND LEAFY 'POT HERBS' SUCH AS SPINACH AND SWISS CHARD WERE AMONG THE FIRST VEGETABLES TO BE CULTIVATED IN EUROPE, AS LONG AGO AS THE STONE AGE. THESE PLANTS CAN BE VERY ATTRACTIVE, AS WELL AS EDIBLE, AND THEY HAVE ENJOYED A RECENT RESURGENCE, REVIVING THE TRADITION OF GROWING VEGETABLES AMONG THE FLOWERS.

Cabbages and sprouts

Using seedbeds or modules Cabbages need to be carefully transplanted or their growth will be checked. Sow seeds into modular trays and transplant them only when the seedlings have developed really strong roots, then harden them off before you plant them. Seedlings that have grown in modules will have well-developed roots and should continue to grow well.

Success with seedlings Plant seedlings to the same depth they were in the seedbed or modular tray. Just before planting, soak the roots of each plant in a mixture of soil and water. When they are growing well, earth them up by drawing soil around the base of each plant. This will ensure the stability of young plants as it encourages them to make new roots along their stems.

Eat up unwanted seedlings Sow cabbage seed into a seedbed, then prick out the seedlings and transplant them into their growing site, where they will have more space to develop.

- Plant a few extra seedlings so you can remove one or two before they mature and use their leaves as spring greens.

What to do with a headless cabbage A cabbage 'head' is formed from layers of leaves folded over each other and is, in effect, a large bud. If a cabbage fails to 'heart up' or make a head, don't leave it to become tough and inedible: remove it and use its foliage as spring greens.

- If any seedlings have not formed proper growing points, get rid of them and replace them with healthy, strong-growing seedlings that will heart up successfully.

Some cabbages are as attractive as they are productive. Plant different varieties together or with ornamental flowers.

Modular trays

COMMERCIAL CABBAGE GROWERS have long used plug plants, and now home growers can raise their seedlings in modular trays as well. The individual plastic cells are ideal for encouraging plants to develop a strong and compact root system so there is minimum root disturbance when they are transplanted and they get off to a good start in the ground. This means that they can often be harvested earlier than nonmodular transplants. Growing your own strong plants from seed will also help to avoid bringing diseases into the vegetable garden.

Get a double crop Instead of pulling out the stumps left in the ground after harvesting cabbages, use a sharp knife to make a cross on the top of each one. Four or five loosely formed heads will sprout from the cross and you will get a second crop.

Preventing club root This is triggered when a microscopic fungus that lives in the soil – and can persist there for decades – finds a host plant to live on. Hygiene is vital, so lift any diseased plants carefully and burn them. Never add plants with club root to the compost heap. You can combat club root with the following cultivational methods.

- **Rotating brassicas** This simple method, deprives the fungus of an appropriate host.
- **Raise the pH level of the soil** The fungus thrives in moist, acid soils, so if you achieve a pH level of 7 or 7.5, it will be too high for the club root fungus to survive. Regularly enrich the soil with lime in the form of powdered chalk, ground limestone or dolomitic limestone. Apply in autumn, so that it acts on the soil before the next growing season begins.
- **Improve drainage** Several months before planting brassicas, dig in a barrowload of well-rotted manure per square metre. To lighten heavy soils, add gravel.

Top tips for growing brassicas Ensure your brassicas have the best possible care by following a few basic rules.

- **Rotate them** Move brassicas around, so that they are never on the same patch more than once every three years. If you grow them in the same spot year after year, you are likely to see a build-up of club root and cabbage root fly. Because they are greedy feeders, the soil needs enriching after they have grown.
- **Stake them** Stake individual Brussels sprout plants and rows of broccoli and kale. Support top-heavy ballhead cabbages and cauliflowers to stop them from lying on the ground.
- **Protect them** Some plants, including tomatoes, are said to repel cabbage white butterfly, so regularly place the suckers pinched out from your tomato plants, or fresh sprigs of broom or fern, on the cabbage leaves. The butterflies dislike the smell of these plants and, it is said, will avoid your cabbage patch.
- **Underplant them** Underplanting cabbages with a green manure may distract insects

Transplanting cabbage seedlings

1 Carefully remove a seedling from its pot or seedbed, use a dibber or trowel to make a hole, and lower the seedling into the planting hole, taking care not to damage the roots.

2 Water the seedling in and use your fingers to firm the soil around the roots. Water well at the base of each plant. Protect young plants from wind and sun by covering with a crate or horticultural fleece. Cutting back leaves by half may reduce evaporation and water loss.

that would otherwise lay their eggs on the cabbage leaves.

Storage Handle winter cabbages carefully when lifting for storage. The roots can be left intact or they can be cut leaving a stump of about 1cm. Store at a temperature close to freezing, in a place where they will not dry out. Laying them on slatted shelves or straw in a cool shed is usually stable

Don't use manure with Brussels sprouts Leafy members of the cabbage family need to be planted in well-manured soil, but not Brussels sprouts since too much nitrogen – one of the main nutrients in manure – will produce open heads, rather than the tightly budded sprouts you are aiming for. If your soil is naturally fertile, you do not need to add any manure to the area where you intend to plant your sprouts. If the soil is infertile, however, add a little well-rotted garden compost.

Using vegetables in your flowerbeds

You can use many plants in the cabbage family to add colour and texture to borders. In recent years, the tradition of growing vegetables for both decorative and practical purposes has regained popularity in many ordinary kitchen gardens and stately homes alike, harking back to a time when good husbandry demanded that every bit of land was cherished.

Ornamental cabbages are especially suitable, and as temperatures drop in autumn, their colours intensify. 'Black Tuscany', a kale also known as the 'palm cabbage', is a spectacular plant with a bouquet of dark, blue-green leaves that can reach a height of up to 2m. Kale is frost-hardy and is especially decorative when its frothy, blue-green or purple leaves are edged with frost.

Removing sprout tops Although Brussels sprouts are tightly packed along the stem, you can twist the buttons off by hand. If you use a knife to remove them, take care not to damage the smaller sprouts nearby.

- When picking a small quantity, take them from the base of the stem and work upwards, as the sprouts higher up the stem will be smaller and mature later than those lower down.
- The leaves at the tops of the sprout stems are good to cook and eat as greens. If you remove these green tops, you are also depriving aphids of potential resting and feeding places.

Try some kale A leafy, cabbage-like vegetable, kale is widely grown in countries throughout northern Europe, but often neglected in British gardens. However, it is worth making space for as it is completely resistant to hard frosts, and although whitefly can be a problem, is relatively unaffected by aphids, caterpillars and other garden pests. Kale is also less prone to club root than cabbages.

- **Sow kale in April or May.** The leaves will be ready to harvest according to your needs after the first frosts, and from then on throughout winter.

Cauliflower and broccoli

Cauliflowers are greedy feeders that thrive in deep, fertile soil and need to be watered regularly. If you live near the sea, gather seaweed from the shore and spread it on the ground before digging over. Alternatively, you can enrich every $10m^2$ of soil with 50kg of compost; 1kg of fish, blood and bone meal; or another natural manure rich in organic nitrogen. Proprietary fertilisers which contain seaweed extracts are also available.

For bright white cauliflowers If a cauliflower head is overexposed to light and bad weather, it loses its pure white colour.

Know your brassicas

The brassica family includes many different types of cabbage, as well as kale, cauliflower, broccoli, kohlrabi (see page 49) and Brussels sprouts.

1 Winter cabbage This ballheaded cabbage has crinkly, textured leaves.
2 Autumn cabbage has smooth, tightly packed leaves.
3 Broccoli Some are green and some have purple sprouts. Though the younger leaves and stalk can be eaten, they are grown for their flower heads.
4 Cauliflower Usually it has a creamy-white flower head surrounded by green leaves but varieties such as 'Purple Cape' have coloured heads.
5 Brussels sprouts Sprouts are mini cabbages growing at leaf points on the stalk. They are plentiful throughout winter.
6 Kale Kale, or borecole, is a nonhearting cabbage with curly, wrinkled leaves.

To protect it and preserve its whiteness, bend the largest outer leaves so that the leaf spine cracks, and fold them over and fix them to cover the head.

Romanesco – gaining in popularity For variety, try planting this delicately flavoured Italian cauliflower. It has an unusual and quite geometric conical shape with pointed, yellow-green florets, but is cultivated like other cauliflowers.

Picking the right moment To get a double crop of broccoli, it needs to be harvested when the flower heads are well formed, but before they open. Examine your broccoli regularly to stop the plants from flowering. Do not allow any flowers to go to seed. To harvest the broccoli, cut the heads off at the top of the stalk. Once you cut off the heads, don't pull up the plant. The buds in the axils of the remaining leaves will develop and provide another crop of smaller heads.

Growing lettuces

Lettuces of every description The word lettuce (*Lactuca sativa*) usually conjures up an image of the lovely, pale green cabbage lettuce. However, lettuces come in all shapes, colours and textures. There are so many different varieties to choose from, you could eat a different one for each day of the week.

- **Butterhead types** These are the most familiar British lettuces. They have soft leaves that heart up into crisp centres, and can be all green or have red-tinged leaves.
- **Crisphead** The tight, crisp, dense heads of these varieties can be green or red-tinged.
- **Cos** (or Romaine) A lettuce with a long conical head, which produces a crisp yellow heart and has deep green outer leaves. Sometimes these are red-tinged.
- **Looseleaf** These lettuces include salad bowl and oakleaf types. They can be used as whole heads, or picked by the leaf.
- **Mixed salad leaf seed collections** A good option for the indecisive, these are attractive in the ground as well as in salad bowls.

American and European varieties The 'Iceberg' lettuce from America is the descendant of the European Batavia lettuce 'Chou de Naples'. It was introduced into California from Italy in the 1920s. Try 'Great Lakes' or one of the European varieties, such as 'Dickenson' or 'Lollo Rosso', whose seeds are more readily available in Britain. The American Batavia lettuces are resistant to hot weather.

Top tips for growing lettuce To make sure your lettuces are tender and juicy, follow these guidelines.

- **Provide moist soil** Grow lettuce in a moisture-retentive soil to prevent the plants from bolting. To increase its water-holding capacity, add compost or manure annually.
- **Use available space** If you're short of space, plant lettuces as a catch crop between sowings of cabbages. The lettuces will be ready to harvest before the cabbages take up all the space.
- **Water correctly** Water lettuces at the base and not in the heart of the plant. If the heart is soaked it may rot.
- **Get rid of weeds** Hoe to keep rows weed-free. There's an old saying, 'Hoeing once is the equivalent of watering twice.' This is because hoeing loosens the soil and lowers the rate of evaporation of moisture and, as weeds are competitors for water, getting rid of them gives the lettuces a better chance.
- **Pick at the right time** To test whether a hearting lettuce is ready to pick, feel the heart – it should be nice and firm. If it is not, leave the plant in the ground for a few days more.

Lettuces on the level When you prick out lettuces, don't plant them too deeply. The point at which the rosette of leaves joins the stem should be above the surface of the soil. Just water in lightly.

Small plug plants of lettuce, beetroot and brassicas are just ready to pot on into larger containers or plant out.

■ When planting lettuce plugs, plant the top just level with the surface of the soil.

Growing lettuce under glass Extend the season by growing lettuce in a protected environment. 'Clarion' (butterhead) and 'Challenge' (crisphead) are two lettuces that can be grown successfully in an unheated greenhouse or cold frame.

Producing your own seeds To harvest seeds, leave one or two plants to go to seed. When the seeds are ripe they look tufty and will start to disperse in the wind. At this stage pull up the plant and hang it upside down in a cool, dry place. Peg large paper bags over the flower heads to catch any seeds that fall from them. Collect the remainder of the seeds by shaking or knocking them into the bag. Clean the seed over winter, carefully removing any dust, earth or other pieces of debris, and store in a cool, dry place ready for use.

Success with seedlings Sow seeds into trays filled with compost, and water them. Once seedlings appear keep the soil moist.

■ When seedlings are established and have good root systems, transplant into larger pots if you want to overwinter them in the greenhouse, or plant them directly into the soil in a greenhouse border. Make sure there is good air circulation in the greenhouse to prevent outbreaks of mildew. Several lettuce varieties, including 'Clarion', have good resistance to mildew.

■ Sow seed early in the growing season to get an early harvest. As soon as the soil warms up and the weather improves, harden seedlings off in a cold frame. If it is an overwinter crop, plant into a cold frame.

Cut-and-come-again lettuce Mixed salad leaf seed collections are useful for colour and variety. They take up less space than other lettuce sowings, and you can get three to four cuts from each one of the plants.

Transplanting lettuce seedlings

1 Use a trowel to lift young seedlings gently from an outdoor seedbed.

2 Hold by the leaves and treat the root carefully. Trimming leaves may help avoid evaporation.

3 Use a dibber to make a hole and lower the seedling into it, so that the leaves are level with the top of the soil. Use your hands to firm the soil around the plant and water it in.

Grow in a partially shaded site and keep the plants well watered. Sow seeds continuously from March to August and harvest as you require the tender young leaves. Try 'Flamenco', which is an oak-leaf type, 'Lollo Rosso' or 'Lollo Bionda'.

Endives, radicchio and chicory

Sharp-tasting salad leaves Endives have deeply cut and loose foliage, which can be blanched by covering or tying the leaves up around the heads. Chicory, also known as Belgian chicory or Witloof, is lifted and forced into producing smooth-leaved, tightly packed heads.

■ Radicchio (red chicory) has marbled red and white foliage. Forcing will give it a less bitter taste.

Preventing bitterness in endives To produce an endive that isn't bitter, you have to prevent the leaves of the heart from turning green by protecting them from the light for about ten days before harvesting. This is called blanching. Make sure the endives are dry, so that the heart doesn't rot, then tie up the head with raffia or rubber ties. Alternatively, place a cloche or dish over the heart of the plant, which will make it stay white.

Chicory is essentially a root The edible part of chicory is the large bud that develops after forcing. Sow chicory seeds in May, in soil that has been well dug over and broken down. It is not advisable to add manure or compost to the area where you grow chicory, since organic matter, as well as hard lumps of earth, will cause the roots to fork. The aim is to produce regularly formed roots that look like parsnips.

Easy-to-grow chicory 'Pain de Sucre', named after the shape and size of its head, is an extremely reliable variety of chicory. This variety does not need to be lifted and blanched. It will heart up in situ and can be harvested and eaten without additional blanching. It produces tender, pale yellow, slightly bitter leaves during autumn and part of winter. The outside leaves will go mushy if temperatures fall below –5°C, but you can

Forcing chicory

1 Dig up the chicory roots in October–November, using a garden fork and taking care not to damage them.Cut off leaves 2cm above the neck: remove hair roots from the main root. The root should be 15–20cm long.

2 Stand the roots point down in a box part-filled with compost. Fill spaces between roots with compost. Place box in a cool, dark place and cover loosely with black plastic. Keep soil moist.

3 Buds will gradually develop in the dark to form small, tightly packed heads. Once the buds are fully grown, harvest the heads as required.

remove these by washing them off and the centre will still be edible.

Spinach and chard

Growing spinach It is simple to grow spinach, in soil that is lightly dug, but there are a couple of things to bear in mind.

- Spinach's worst enemy is damping-off, a disease caused by the parasitic fungus Pythium debaryanum. This persists in the soil, lying dormant until damp conditions and the right host – spinach seedlings – are available. Formerly gardeners attempted to prevent this by sprinkling powdered charcoal in the drill when sowing seeds. However, it can be avoided by ensuring that you space the seedlings so that there is a good current of air.
- Spinach grows best when there are equal amounts of daylight and darkness, so it thrives in spring and autumn. Sow in March, April or September.

Easy to grow New Zealand spinach (*Tetragonia expansa*) has distinctive diamond-shaped leaves. Sow in March, under glass, or outdoors in May, after soaking the seeds for 24 hours. Plant three or four seeds per module or in planting holes in the ground spaced 70cm apart.

The plants will spread and produce continuously from July to October. Harvest the leaves carefully without damaging the main stem.

Chard, also called leaf chard or leaf beet, is a large leafy vegetable, as ornamental in the kitchen and flower garden as it is delicious in cooking. There are red-stemmed and yellow-stemmed (right), varieties, as well as those with green, mixed and rainbow-coloured stems and leaves.
The leaves and stalks have a pungent, earthy flavour and are delicious served with a white sauce or butter. The white-stemmed variety, also known as seakale beet, Swiss chard or perpetual spinach has green leaves and white or green stems. A tip for harvesting is to twist the stalk as you pull.

Enrich the soil with nitrogen Take advantage of spinach's production of nitrogen in its leaves and use any surplus seeds or plants as an alternative green manure. Sow spinach at the end of summer in any uncultivated areas of the vegetable garden. The first frosts will kill the plants. Then simply dig them in just below the surface, and the nitrogen in the spinach leaves will enrich the soil.

Plant a number of different varieties of chard – the coloured stems will provide a lively display in a vegetable garden.

26 Legumes and sweetcorn

BEANS AND PEAS BELONG TO THE LEGUME FAMILY, LONG CULTIVATED BY GARDENERS AS USEFUL SOIL IMPROVERS BECAUSE OF THE WAY THEY ABSORB NITROGEN. THEY FIX IT IN NODULES ON THEIR ROOTS AND SO FEED THE SOIL WHEN THEY ROT. SWEETCORN, ON THE OTHER HAND, IS A RELATIVE NEWCOMER AND A GREEDY FEEDER.

Purple-podded dwarf French beans should be harvested every two to three days before the seeds swell and the pods get stringy.

Growing beans

French beans and runner beans Sow seed in soil that has been well manured the previous autumn or winter. These beans need warmth and moisture to germinate, so wait until late spring when the ground has warmed up. Add runner beans, with their colourful flowers, to a flower border.

Earthing up Old-fashioned gardeners found that earthing up dwarf French beans helps to support the stems, so that the bean plants can establish well. It also maintains moisture around the roots.

Sow French beans in succession French beans are sown from mid April to July and harvested from June onwards. If you sow them in succession you will have crops at regular intervals, rather than needing to harvest everything at once.

- Times between sowing and harvesting vary, depending on the type of bean, but generally allow 7–13 weeks (up to 16 weeks for climbing beans). Using this rough guide

Planting runner beans

1 Plant beans sown under glass in spring 15cm apart in double rows 60cm apart.

2 Install a cane support structure and secure it well before the beans start to grow tall.

3 Start guiding the stems up a line or wigwam of bamboo canes from inside the structure.

you can gauge how many sowings you need to make during the growing season.

Runner beans keep on cropping For runner beans, sow from May to July and harvest from July onwards. You don't need to make successional sowings of runner beans, just keep picking the beans regularly to ensure continuous flowering and therefore bean production.

■ Water runner beans regularly to keep them cropping.

Saving bean seeds Allow the last beans on each plant – those that are too high to harvest – to ripen fully. The pods will turn yellow and begin to look dry and shrivelled. At this point, pick them and remove the beans from the pods. Store them in paper bags in a cool, frost-free, dry place. Label the bags with the name of the bean and the following year you can sow them.

■ You can also save seed from broad beans and peas. Don't save seed taken from F1 hybrids as they will not come true to type.

Feed runner beans on waste Because they produce their own nitrogen, runner beans can digest uncomposted material. In early spring, when you are tidying the garden, fill a trench with the soft greenery and harmless weeds that you have just cleared from elsewhere on your plot.

■ When it is time to plant, chop up these cuttings with a spade, cover them with compost-enriched soil, and either sow runner bean seeds or plant young seedlings.

Conserving moisture Although preparing the soil well by digging in uncomposted green waste and well-rotted manure helps to keep the ground damp, take other measures to further reduce the need for watering in dry spells. A mulch of compost or black plastic sheeting will help to lock in moisture.

Stringless beans

Runner beans have 'strings' running down the pod, which can become tough with age. New varieties of beans, including 'Delinel', are especially popular because they are stringless. 'Berggold', a yellow-skinned variety, is a tasty stringless bean, as is 'Opera', a Kenyan variety. Many of the new varieties are resistant to diseases including common bean mosaic virus, halo blight and anthracnose.

Broad beans

Easy to grow in most soil conditions, sowing broad beans couldn't be simpler.

■ **Early sowing** Make the first outdoor sowing early in March and follow with sowings in late March and April. Place seeds in a drill at a depth of 3–4cm, at intervals of about 20cm. They will germinate in two or three weeks. Some varieties can be sown later, though many gardeners say that these late-sown beans are more susceptible to blackfly and give a lower yield.

■ **Autumn sowing** Several varieties, such as 'The Sutton' and 'Aquadulce Claudia', can be sown in late autumn from October through to December, then overwintered, and harvested in May or June. Pick them as soon as the pods are full and the beans appear swollen: the younger the bean, the more tender it will be.

Beans can be sown directly into the ground. Set them 2–3cm deep and 15cm apart.

An early start for peas

Under cloches Warm up the soil with cloches two weeks before sowing outdoors. Sow runner beans and French beans in April for a July crop. Sow broad beans in early March for an early June crop. Sow peas in late February for a June crop. Protect sowings and seedlings with cloches until all danger of frost has passed.

Cold frames and greenhouses Sow runner beans in a cold frame in early April using heat to force germination. Sow French beans in a cold frame in late March; harden off in May. Sow broad beans in a cold frame as early as January; harden off in March. Sow early wrinkled-seed peas in February (if temperatures are 7–10°C); harden off in March.

■ **Broad beans need support** Tall varieties of broad bean may need support if grown in exposed sites. Tie the plants to individual canes or, to support a whole row of beans, use two stakes with a fork at the top, inserted firmly into the soil at either end of the row. Lay a bamboo cane across from fork to fork and tie it in. Then, at intervals, tie into this horizontal cane upright canes which will support the beans as they grow.

Give peas a head start

1 Start peas in cold areas by sowing in a length of plastic guttering filled with seed compost.

2 Slide the 'instant' row of peas into a shallow trench outdoors when weather conditions allow.

Pinching out tops Broad beans often attract aphids. Pinching out the tops, where the youngest and tastiest shoots are found, may rid the plants of the pest. Pinching out will also stop the plants from getting leggy.

Perfect peas

The best time for sowing Peas should be sown in succession according to the following timetable for outdoor sowing. Sugar snap peas can be harvested very early, as the peas don't develop fully.

- **First earlies** Sow March–June, harvest 11–13 weeks later.
- **Second earlies** Sow March–June, harvest 13–14 weeks later.
- **Maincrop** Sow March–June, harvest 14–15 weeks later.

Sow peas deep The first two seed leaves develop below ground, so peas have to be sown at a depth of about 5cm in order to develop a good root system. They also need to be densely planted, so sow seeds close together, no more than 1–2cm apart.

Round peas To produce a good crop, round garden peas need to be cool. Sow between February and April. Try 'Feltham First', 'Oregon Sugar Pod' and 'Meteor', which can also be sown in autumn and overwintered.

Wrinkled peas Wrinkled varieties of peas are sweeter and firmer than the round types when cooked. They are also more resistant to hot weather and can be harvested for a longer period. They are sown between the end of March and May and include varieties such as 'Kelvedon Wonder', 'Little Marvel', 'Hurst Green Shaft' and 'Onward'.

Staking peas All types of peas are climbers and need support for their twining tendrils. The most popular kind comes from sticks, known as 'pea sticks', which are twiggy branches often cut from hazel bushes that are coppiced in winter.

■ It is easier to stake and harvest peas when grown in double rows 50–75cm apart.

Succulent sweetcorn

Plant sweetcorn in blocks Sweetcorn must be wind-pollinated It has two sets of flowers: male flowers are the long tassels at the top of the plant, and female flowers are the 'silks' below which the cobs develop. Pollen is blown from the male flowers to pollinate the female flowers, so planting in blocks rather than rows favours pollination.

Sweetcorn needs warm weather to establish itself. Sow direct once there is no danger of frost and the soil has warmed up – not before early June.

■ **Sow two or three seeds** in holes about 3cm deep and 25–30cm apart. For a greater success rate, sow two or three kernels in a pot, and transplant seedlings out into the garden when all danger of frost has passed.

■ As plants grow, lateral roots may develop at the soil surface. Leave them in place, as they anchor and nourish the plants.

Harvest time The 'silks' will tell you when it is time to harvest. Initially green, when the silks have turned dark brown, and look and feel dry, the cob is ripe.

■ Check ripeness by peeling back the bracts. Before they mature, the kernels are milky and translucent. When ripe, they should be plump and tender – test with your thumbnail – and bright yellow, pale cream or black.

Sowing and planting sweetcorn

1 Sow seeds of sweetcorn individually in biodegradable peat pots in a heated greenhouse.

2 Peat pots must not be allowed to dry out, so stand them in a tray of water, which is slowly taken up from the bottom. When they are in the ground, the roots will grow through the base.

3 Plant sweetcorn seedlings in a block, 35cm apart in each direction.The wind will pollinate the block-grown plants once they flower.

30 Fruiting vegetables

TOMATOES, MARROWS AND MELONS SWELL WITH THE PROMISE OF A SUCCULENT MATURITY. ONCE THESE RAMPANT GROWERS WERE CONFINED TO THE GREENHOUSE, BUT NOW IMPROVED VARIETIES AND TECHNIQUES MEAN THAT MOST CAN BE GROWN OUTDOORS.

There is nothing as delicious as home-grown, vine-ripened tomatoes. Pick them regularly as they ripen.

Growing tomatoes

Seeds need heat Tomato seeds need warmth to germinate. Sow into seed compost in trays or modules in a heated propagator in January or February. Transplant into larger pots when they have produced three to four leaves. Harden off outdoor varieties, and plant indoor varieties in growbags in the greenhouse.

Staking tomatoes Push stakes firmly into the ground, leaving 60cm between each, so that the plants have enough room to grow. Make a planting hole about 10cm in front of each stake and place plants into the holes, angling them slightly towards the stakes. Water the plants in and then gently firm the soil, taking care not to damage the stems. As the plants grow, begin to tie them against the stakes to support them. Do this regularly, especially with cordon-type tomatoes.

Water reservoirs Tomatoes need regular and copious watering. To make sure they get enough, sink a small flower pot into the ground near the base of each cane. Pour water into this every day so that it fills up and then slowly drains into the soil near the plants. Or remove the top from the neck of a 2-litre plastic bottle, cut the bottle in half and sink the neck into the ground. Fill with water every day.

- During the growing season, tomatoes need regular feeding, so use this reservoir for applying water-soluble fertiliser. You can also feed the plants with liquid manure made from nettle or comfrey.

Mulching is essential Tomato plants need to be well spaced because of their volume. It is a good idea to cover the soil at their base with a mulch. Use straw, the foliage of comfrey or nettle plants, or chipped bark, in a layer up to 5cm deep. This suppresses weeds and helps to prevent water loss from the soil surface. Mulch only on damp soil to keep the existing moisture in, otherwise it will prevent the rain reaching the roots and ensure that dry soil simply stays dry.

Cordon tomato plants have a naturally trailing or climbing habit and most need

Plant out tomatoes when all danger of frost is past. For protection, cover the young plants with a cloche or a layer of horticultural fleece.

some support. Training them upwards means they escape the adverse effects of damp soil – a potential disease risk.

■ Use hazel poles or canes, at least 1.5m long, pushed into the ground near the base of each plant. As the plants grow, tie the stems to the stakes with string.

■ To ensure that the stakes are stable, arrange them in groups of three or four, angled towards the centre, and tie firmly at the top to form a wigwam shape for the plants to grow on.

Bush types Some varieties of tomato, such as the 'Roma', have a bushy habit and don't need staking, However, in a garden, it's a good idea to keep these varieties off the ground to prevent their fruits from rotting. Support them on an upturned crate.

Mixed cropping Tomatoes grow well with asparagus, celery, French beans, onions, parsley, leeks and potatoes.

■ Tomatoes don't grow well with cucumber, fennel, peas and beetroot.

■ Plant marigolds (*Calendula*) around them to reduce infestations of whitefly.

Trimming and pinching out Check cordon tomato plants regularly during their early development, and pinch out little shoots that

The pick of the tomato crop

Varieties of tomatoes differ in size, shape, flavour, texture, the colour of the fruit, type of skin (smooth or ribbed), picking time and mildew tolerance. So how do you choose between them?

■ If you like stuffed tomatoes, go for large-fruited varieties.

■ If you are adventurous and like something a bit different, try growing the lesser-known and more unusually coloured or shaped 'heirloom' varieties.

Black Russian An heirloom variety with a dark skin and a good-flavoured flesh.

Big Boy F1 A large, smooth, blemish-free beefsteak-type fruit with thick meaty flesh.

Brandywine Another heirloom, a large-fruited, beefsteak-type with good flavour.

Crimson Fancy F1 A reliable producer, even for inexperienced growers.

Dombito A tasty beefsteak tomato.

Gardener's Delight A late variety with small, very tasty fruits.

Green Sausage A bush tomato with yellow stripes and a green flesh which grows well in a container.

Ildi A very prolific cherry tomato that produces large trusses of yellow oval or pear-shaped fruit.

Marmande and **Super-Marmande** Early heirloom varieties with very large fruits.

Polish Linguisa An old heirloom variety dating from the 1800s, which produces unusual-shaped, large, sweet fruits.

Roma An elongated plum tomato, ideal for making tomato sauces and pizzas.

Striped Stuffer Best grown under glass, with stripes on its skin. It is good for stuffing.

Super Marzano F1 A giant, disease-resistant pear-shaped fruit.

Super Sweet 100 F1 One of the cherry tomatoes that produces red or yellow, sometimes pear-shaped, fruit.

appear in the axils of the leaves. If this is not done the plant will use its energy to become bushy and fruit production will be reduced. Do not pinch out side shoots on bush tomatoes, as they will eventually bear fruit.

A booster shot for tomatoes When your tomatoes begin to bloom, mix two tablespoons of Epsom salts in 5 litres of water and pour onto the soil around the plants. The magnesium and sulphur in the salts encourage healthy fruits.

Hasten ripening In late summer and early autumn, remove any foliage that may be shading the fruit from the sun.

Basking in reflected light Use backing boards to reflect light onto sun-loving tomatoes. Cover a board with aluminium foil, prop it against a support and angle it so that it catches the sun's rays and bounces them onto the ripening fruit.

Making the most of suckers You may notice that tomato suckers, like the other green parts of the plant, have a very pungent smell. This is released – at the slightest contact – as a smelly, coloured substance from many tiny glands on the surface of the plant. Some gardeners say that this property can be used to protect other vegetables against garden pests. For example, it is said that if you place tomato suckers on the leaves of cabbages or other brassicas, the smell of the tomato will disorientate cabbage white butterflies and cabbage moths. This prevents them from laying their eggs on the leaves and protects your brassicas from caterpillar damage.

Ripening after picking In autumn, if tomatoes are slow to ripen outdoors, you may have to pick the crop to avoid frost damage. Bring them into a dry, frost-free room and store them in brown paper bags, newspaper or fruit boxes. You will find that they ripen up in due course. If they don't, use them in green tomato chutneys.

Producing your own tomato seeds Nothing could be easier than producing your own tomato seeds, provided they come from a traditional variety and not an F1 hybrid. Put the pulp of a ripe tomato into a bowl and add a little water. A whitish bacterial film will soon form on the surface of the liquid. After about 36 hours, add more water and

Training tomatoes

1 When growing tomatoes as single-stemmed cordons, anchor the string beneath the rootball and attach it to an overhead wire or the top of the greenhouse roof.

2 Tie the stems to the strings as they grow, or simply twist the string round the stem. (You can also use canes.)

3 Don't forget to snap off all sideshoots from the base of the leaves when they are about 2–5cm long.

stir the mixture – this fermentation process separates the seeds from the pulp, and the seeds will sink to the bottom. Strain off the liquid through a sieve, rinse the seeds under the tap and leave them to dry on a piece of kitchen paper.

A bold splash of colour in the vegetable garden is one of the bonuses of growing pumpkins.

Marrows, courgettes, pumpkins and squash

All in the family Vegetable marrows, courgettes, summer and winter squashes, pumpkins and ornamental (nonedible) gourds are all members of the gourd family *Cucurbitaceae*.

■ Pumpkins and squash are sometimes referred to as winter fruits. They are harvested late in autumn and can be stored in cool, dry conditions through winter. The skins of pumpkin and squash, when ripe, develop a tough exterior and are usually orange, stripey or blue-grey. Their flesh is rich in vitamin C. Pumpkins are less flavoursome than squash, which has a nutty flavour and a finer texture.

■ Marrows, courgettes and summer squash are usually harvested earlier in the growing season and do not keep as long as winter squash. Their skins are softer and their flesh has a blander taste.

Easy to grow Sow courgettes, marrows and pumpkins in situ, allowing 1m between plants in all directions and 2m for trailing varieties. Sow to a depth of about 2cm. Don't sow until late May or early June, when all danger of frost is past.

Long-season courgettes So that you have a plentiful supply of courgettes during summer, sow them in succession between the months of April and July.

■ Sow seeds indoors in April, plant out in late May and harvest from July onwards.

■ Sow seeds direct into the ground in June and harvest from late July onwards.

Two's company Courgettes – which are simply young marrows – are extremely prolific, so don't plant out more than two at a time. Create a hollow around the base of young plants for watering. It will hold water and ensure that it gets to the right spot.

Hand-pollinate squash (above) and pumpkin flowers to ensure good cropping. The plants will produce fruits only if cross-pollinated.

Multicoloured courgettes Courgettes come in a range of colours. As well as the traditional dark green variety, you can grow light green or yellow courgettes.

For an early start use plug plants You can either buy plug plants, or raise seedlings under glass. Plant out towards the end of June, or sow seeds direct into the ground in late May or early June once you are sure there is no frost risk.

Turk's Turban is a colourful and shapely squash with a tasty flesh but it is usually grown for its eyecatching appearance.

Keep weeds down If you plant trailing varieties of marrows, pumpkins and squashes, they will soon cover a vast area with their abundant foliage. Reap the benefit of the foliage keeping the weeds down. To give them somewhere to trail and keep them out of the way, place an old wooden ladder against a fence or wall. Plant trailing varieties at the feet of the ladder, and they will climb up the rungs.

Easy neighbours Courgettes, marrows, squash and pumpkins will grow anywhere, even in poorly prepared soil. If you are starting a new vegetable garden and haven't had time to prepare the ground fully, you can still get a good crop. As long as you can add well-rotted manure to the soil they will thrive almost wherever you plant them.

■ All of these vegetable fruits will do best if planted in a sheltered, sunny position.

Sowing on the compost heap Marrows, squashes and pumpkins need plenty of organic matter and thrive if sown or planted directly on the compost heap. Sometimes they even grow without the help of the gardener since the seeds in kitchen waste often germinate unaided. As an added bonus, the foliage of most pumpkin and squash will provide a natural and attractive covering to keep the compost heap shaded and moist. If the seeds are from F1 hybrids the results may be variable, as the pumpkins won't come true to type.

Top tips for pumpkins and squash Many of these tips will work for tomatoes and cucumbers too.

■ **Encourage more fruits** Nip out the growing tips of the main shoots of trailing plants when they are 45cm long, to promote the growth of lateral shoots and female flowers.

■ **Help pollination** If the fruits are not setting well, pollinate the plants by hand. Use a small brush to transfer pollen from the male flowers to the female, which you can identify by a swelling just behind the bloom.

■ **Remove some leaves** As soon as a small pumpkin develops, remove some of the leaves on the fruit-bearing stem, leaving two or three just above the fruit.

■ **Foil pests** If you spread aluminium foil on the soil around the base of the plants, you can prevent viruses transmitted by thrips and aphids. You can deter cutworm by wrapping stems in a sleeve of aluminium foil, making sure the sleeve is buried 2–3cm in the soil. Taping foil behind the plants, on a fence or wall not only increases light but also confuses pests.

Storing marrows Harvest and store marrows for up to three months in an airy, frost-free place. Many old-fashioned gardeners stored their prize marrows singly in nets hung up in sheds, to keep them from coming into contact with other fruits over the winter storage period.

When to harvest

Fruiting vegetables will be ready to harvest at different times and in varying quantities.

- **Marrows** Harvest as required. Up to 24 fruits can be taken from one plant if they are picked when 30cm long. Leave the last two or three fruits on the plants until October, when they will be fully grown and well ripened.
- **Courgettes** Pick courgettes when they are about 15cm long. The more you pick the more fruits the plant will produce. If they are picked at this size they will be very tasty. Any larger and they are half-way to becoming marrows.
- **Pumpkins and squash** The fruits are ready to pick when they have coloured well and developed a hard skin. Give them a tap and, if they sound hollow, they are ready to pick. Another indicator of ripeness is that the foliage begins to turn brown.

Curing pumpkins and squash After picking, keep the harvested fruit in a sunny place, or indoors in a conservatory or greenhouse, for about ten days so that their skins harden off well. If you are curing them outdoors bring them indoors if frost is forecast.

Storing pumpkins Blemish-free pumpkins will keep for up to three months in a frost-free environment. For maximum protection, store them on relatively warm surfaces, such as wood, cardboard or several layers of newspaper rather than cold surfaces such as stone or cement.

Space invaders In a small garden, avoid trailing marrows, squashes and pumpkins. Some of these varieties can spread for several metres on either side of the main plant and may smother other plants with their huge leaves. Check on the seed packet to see whether varieties are trailing or not.

- Most pumpkins are trailing, especially 'Atlantic Giant', so instead use 'Cinderella', a bush variety. Marrows are generally trailing, but many courgettes are bush varieties. Squashes that form bushy plants, include the nontrailing 'Kaboucha' or the semibush butternut.

Cucumbers and melons

You can grow cucumbers in a greenhouse or outdoors. Indoor cucumbers crop earlier, need to be trained and produce long, succulent fruits. Greenhouse cultivars such 'Futura F1' or 'Telegraph Improved' can also be grown in frames. There are many outdoor varieties including 'Burpless Tasty Green F1'. These varieties tolerate cooler conditions and produce shorter fruits.

Sow indoor cucumbers in March or April, into pots in a frost-free greenhouse. Transplant into frames or the greenhouse border in late spring or early summer. Water the plants well, especially while they are flowering.

Outdoor cucumbers can be grown up canes or along the ground. Remove growing points of stems regularly to encourage bushy

Cucumbers grown in the greenhouse need to be carefully trained to ensure maximum production of fruit.

growth and better fruit setting. After planting in a greenhouse, 'pinch out' the growing tip above the first three or four leaves. This will cause two fruit-bearing shoots to appear in the leaf axils. Tie these shoots onto canes.

Most new greenhouse hybrids are all female and must be unfertilised to prevent a bitter flavour. However, if these plants are stressed by high temperatures or insufficient moisture, they may produce male flowers, which lack the immature cucumber present behind the petals of female flowers. Remove any male flowers from the plants.

Harvest cucumbers when they are a good size but before they turn yellow.

Ridge cucumbers Small outdoor cucumbers are easy to grow and modern varieties are not bitter or as thick skinned as they used to be. Gherkins are the immature fruits of these outdoor ridge cucumbers, usually picked at 8cm or shorter and pickled in vinegar and spices.

Growing melons under cover Sweet melons are trailing plants. They come from warm regions and in our climate are tender. They need plenty of well-rotted manure and should be grown under cover in a cold frame or unheated greenhouse. To get a well-structured plant with good fruits you need to train the plant. Pinch out the leading stem above the second leaf, and pinch out the new shoots that arise above the third leaf. Then, when melons appear, pinch out the stems two leaves above the fruits, and support them with netting.

Sow melons in spring and early summer direct into the greenhouse or cold frame soil, but remember the seeds need a minimum temperature of 16°C to germinate. The plants will thrive if a temperature of 20°C can be guaranteed.

Support young melons with 'hammocks' or bags of soft plastic netting or muslin. Pick when the stem cracks at the base of the fruit.

Watering Melons need regular and copious water especially when in flower so that good fruits develop. They need plenty of nutrients so use a tomato fertiliser with added magnesium.

Keep pollinating insects out until it's time As soon as the first melon fruits set, no others will develop, so you need to keep pollinating insects away from the flowers until all of them – or enough for your needs – have fully opened. To keep insects out use cloches or fleece over the plants, then once the flowers are open lift the cloches or fleece and allow the insects access. They will pollinate the flowers and you will have a number of fruits ripening at the same time.

Traditional hotbeds This old-fashioned method gives all fruiting vegetables, including marrows and cucumbers, a good start. Before planting, dig out a bed and fill it with organic matter which, as it decomposes, releases heat and helps the plants to develop. (In the old days, this would have been fresh manure as it was widely available, but any organic matter will work.) Cover the organic matter with a good layer of soil, and sow or plant into that. The soil cover prevents heat loss from the hotbed and protects the young plants, which might otherwise rot due to the heat and moisture from the heap. For a finishing touch, you could cover each plant with a cloche.

Aubergines and peppers

As a native of the tropical regions of Asia, the aubergine requires a great deal of heat to grow well, and so they are best grown here under glass.

■ If you are tempted to try to grow aubergines outdoors, however, plant them from mid May onwards on a sunny site, sheltered from the north wind. If necessary, protect young plants with cloches.

■ 'Moneymaker', 'Black Enorma', 'Violet Pearl' and 'Bonica F1' are among the best varieties.

Restricting growth for an early harvest

You need to force aubergines into producing flowers as early as possible. To do this, pinch out the growing point once the plant has produced up to five leaves, taking it out above the fifth leaf. Soon flowers will be produced by the lateral shoots, which you should also pinch out above their fourth leaves. This second pinching-out will force the plant to put all its energy into producing fruit, which you will be able to harvest earlier than if the plant was left to grow its own way.

Pepper pots Peppers need warmth to grow and normally have to be planted in a greenhouse to crop well. However, if you have a warm spot try a pepper in a 30cm pot supported by a cane. Pinch out the growing point when the plant is 15cm tall and water well. If growing in a greenhouse, mist regularly to increase the humidity. Use a foliar feed of diluted seaweed solution and guard against slugs, which love the fruit.

■ For the largest peppers grow 'Big Bertha', or try 'Californian Wonder' or 'Canape'.

Aubergines thrive in the border of a greenhouse. You may be able to grow them outdoors in very mild areas.

Stars of the pepper family

The capsicum or pepper plant can be divided into two types: the sweet (bell) type and the hot (chilli) type. The larger sweet peppers have a milder taste. Grow all types in a greenhouse, or in milder areas try a few in a pot on a sunny patio. Water them well in hot weather.

Purple Beauty An unusual deep-purple colour, it is sweet and juicy straight off the plant.
Minibel A newly developed variety.
Jalapeño This classic American hot chilli pepper is used on pizzas.
Cherry Pick This produces small, round fruits, on vigorous, disease-resistant plants.
Habañero A very hot pepper used in curries and other spicy dishes.
Corno di Toro This is a long pepper which can be red or yellow. It is great stuffed, stir-fried or eaten raw.

38 Perennial vegetables

ASPARAGUS, JERUSALEM ARTICHOKES, GLOBE ARTICHOKES AND RHUBARB ARE ALL PERENNIAL VEGETABLES WITH AN ENDURING APPEAL FOR SELF-SUFFICIENT GARDENERS. ONCE THE STARTER PLANTS ARE WELL SETTLED INTO THE KITCHEN GARDEN, THEY WILL GO ON PRODUCING PLENTIFUL CROPS INDEFINITELY.

Asparagus is harvested just below ground level when the tips are about 7-10cm above the ground.

Asparagus

Light, sandy soils are ideal for growing asparagus. When preparing an asparagus bed, lighten the soil with nonacidic river sand, available from garden centres.

- To plant in spring, prepare the ground in autumn by digging over and adding compost or well-rotted manure (about 50kg per 10m^2) and a complete organic fertiliser (30–40g per m^2). Remove weeds as asparagus plants must not have competition, but do not hoe or they will not thrive.
- After harvesting, spread compost or manure on the asparagus bed and cut back old stems to soil level once they have turned yellow or brown.

Planting asparagus crowns

1 Dig a trench 45cm deep and incorporate plenty of well-rotted organic matter. Make a shallow ridge down the centre.

2 Plant crowns 10–15cm deep, spreading out roots either side of the ridge. Space 30cm apart in rows 45cm apart. Earth over the trench and add compost. In heavy soils, plant more shallowly, but earth up the stems as they grow.

Choosing the sex of your asparagus Asparagus is a 'dioecious perennial'. That is, plants have either male or female flowers. Male plants produce more vigorous shoots, but you'll have to trust your supplier, since the only way to distinguish female plants is by their red berries in summer.

Harvesting asparagus The knack to harvesting asparagus is to cut it off at an angle with a sharp knife, just below ground level. Asparagus is ready to harvest in April and May when the tips of the young, green shoots are 10–15cm long.

■ Asparagus is best harvested after its second or third year, when the roots of the plant have become well established in the soil. If you start harvesting shoots too soon, you'll weaken the plant and possibly affect the next year's harvest.

Globe artichokes

Start out with offshoots Nurseries and garden centres sell young artichokes in pots. If you can find a gardener who grows artichokes, ask for some offshoots in April or May. To remove these from the clump, separate some strong-looking shoots from the main plant with a garden spade. The shoots must have rootlets at the base. Cut back the leaves to half their length and plant immediately, leaving 80cm between plants.

Bigger artichokes
As soon as young artichokes form, pierce the stem, just below the flower head, with a pointed piece of wood. No one knows the science of this tip, but the fact remains that the artichokes grow bigger as a result.
■ As they develop, leave just four to six flower heads on each plant. By limiting the number of heads, you are preventing the plant from exhausting its reserves.
■ For tender artichokes, the bud must grow rapidly. Water regularly, especially in dry weather, mulch and add manure.

Jerusalem artichokes

Once in the garden, Jerusalem artichokes are there for ever. When you harvest, it is impossible to remove all the tubers, and so some remain in the ground, ready to be next year's crop. Jerusalem artichokes grow up to 3m tall, so place them where you have space for a permanent stand. Make the most of their height and get extra value by using them as a sheltering windbreak in the vegetable garden.

Dependable performers Jerusalem artichokes grow well on most soils in sun or shade. Plant tubers in spring to a depth of 10–15cm, about 30cm apart, and harvest from late autumn through winter.
■ The variety 'Fuseau' has long, white tubers that resemble certain potato varieties. 'Dwarf Sunray' produces tubers that do not need to be peeled.

Rhubarb is classified as a vegetable but its stalks are eaten as a fruit. The leaves should never be eaten as they are poisonous.

Rhubarb

Instant rhubarb If you want to be able to harvest rhubarb soon after planting, don't buy plants in pots at a garden centre – they take years to mature. Instead, in March, ask someone with an established patch of good-quality rhubarb for some healthy pieces of root with one or two buds for propagation. Dividing the roots of old clumps of rhubarb revives and reinvigorates them so there are benefits for both of you.

Keep it cool All rhubarb needs is a cool – even damp – place in the sun or semi-shade. It doesn't need protection against frost in winter, even in the coldest regions.

To harvest rhubarb without breaking the stems, twist them slightly and then pull gently.
■ If you harvest rhubarb regularly it will not flower. The flowers are not unattractive, but the plant puts its energy into producing them rather than the leaf stalks so cut out any developing flower stems.

Growing root vegetables

THE PROVIDENT GARDENER WAS ONCE JUDGED ON THE RICHNESS OF HIS WINTER RESERVES. SO IT IS HARDLY SURPRISING THAT EASY-TO-STORE BEETROOT, CARROTS AND TURNIPS WERE, AND STILL ARE, MAINSTAYS OF THE KITCHEN GARDEN. SUPPLEMENT THEM WITH FAST-GROWING RADISHES, PARSNIPS, SWEDE AND TRY A LITTLE CELERIAC.

Winter-hardy beetroot

The two main varieties of beetroot are the globe and the long-rooted.

- **The globe beetroot** The familiar round beetroot is less prone to bolting than other varieties and can be sown several weeks earlier, to provide roots from June. 'Avonearly', 'Boltardy' and 'Early Bunch' are recommended. For later sowings to provide roots for autumn and early winter use, sow the small-rooted, quick-growing 'Little Ball'.
- **The long-rooted types** This variety is still frequently used for a main crop that is allowed to mature in the ground before being harvested and stored in early winter. 'Cheltenham Green Top' is a good variety. 'Cylindra' is another long-rooted variety, which is easy to prepare for cooking.

Traditional cultivation Beetroots thrive on light soil, but will grow successfully on most fertile, well-cultivated vegetable patches. Sow seed thinly in rows 30cm apart. Barely cover with soil and water in well. Thin out as seedlings develop to a spacing of 15cm between plants.

A harvest you can leave in the ground
Beetroot is grown to be harvested any time from June into early winter, depending on the variety.

- As soon as they are large enough to cook, you can pull up early globes whenever you need them.
- Main crops for winter use can be left in the ground until required if they are covered with straw or bracken to protect them from frost. Alternatively, you can lift them in November and store in boxes of sand in a frost proof shed, or outdoors in a clamp (see page 43). Cut the tops off the roots for storing, being careful not to cut too close to the crown or the root will bleed.

A fast-maturing crop, beetroot can produce gluts and gaps. Avoid this by sowing small amounts of seed at regular intervals.

A visual feast If you like decorative dishes and a touch of originality, grow yellow beetroot, such as 'Golden', or even two-tone beetroot with concentric circles of red and white, such as 'Pink Chioggia'. You should be able to buy the seeds from most good vegetable seed catalogues.

Carrots for all seasons

For best results grow carrots in light or sandy soils. The ground needs careful preparation before you can sow them. Fork the soil and rake out all stones and debris. Also remove perennial weeds.

■ Carrots can develop long taproots, depending on variety, and need to be able to grow straight down into the soil. If you don't prepare the soil well, the result will be carrots that are forked or otherwise misshapen.

Growing in heavy soil You can get round this problem by growing short or intermediate varieties in raised beds. Break down the soil with the back of a rake, then build up long ridges about 10cm deep and 30–40cm wide. Sow the carrot seeds, preferably coated (see page 46) as they are so small, into their ridges. You may also need to install a seep hose system for economical watering as these ridged beds dry out very quickly.

Carrot shapes There are short-rooted, almost round carrots for growing in the smallest spaces, intermediate carrots and long-rooted carrots with tapering roots. Short-rooted carrots are harvested relatively early. They are tender but less productive than the other types.

■ **Short-rooted carrots**, harvested in early summer, include 'Parmex' and 'Parabel'.

■ **Intermediate-rooted 'earlies'**, harvested in summer or autumn, include 'Early Nantes', 'Early Scarlet Horn' and 'Amsterdam Forcing III'.

■ **Intermediate-rooted 'lates'**, harvested in late autumn, include 'Flyaway F1' and 'Royal Chantenay 2', which are shorter and well suited to heavy, shallow soils.

■ **Long-rooted carrots**, harvested in late autumn, include 'St Valery', 'Kingston F1' and 'Autumn King 2', which are suitable for light soils and have a high yield.

Yields from root crops

While a poor harvest is disappointing, it can be equally problematic to produce more vegetables than you can use. It is best to know what to expect, so here is the average yield per square metre of some popular root vegetables.

Carrots 1–3.5kg
Celeriac approximately 7 roots
Radishes 500 radishes
Salsify 2–3kg
Turnips (spring) 50–100 mini-turnips
Turnips (autumn) approximately 3kg

Don't let weeds take over Carrots are slow to germinate and weeds can soon take over the bed. This is why carrots have a reputation for being a 'messy' crop. It can be tricky trying to pull up weeds without uprooting the carrots.

■ There is a partial solution to the problem – mock sowings. Prepare the soil as if you were going to sow your carrot seeds, but don't actually sow them. Wait for it to rain and for the weeds to come through. As soon as the soil dries out, uproot the young weeds

Carrots thrive particularly well in a friable soil with a fine, uniform texture and no stones or hard lumps.

with a rake. Repeat the process a few days later, when the soil is dry, then sow your carrot seeds for real.

Pre-germination Cover carrot seeds with warm water and leave them to soak overnight. If you have a sprouting jar for mung beans, use it to 'pre-germinate' the seeds for 48 hours and then sow immediately – don't let them dry out.

Sowing sparsely According to an old saying, if you sow seeds thickly you'll have a sparse harvest. This is particularly true of carrots, whose fine seeds are difficult to sow evenly in the drill. The ideal spacing would be one seed every 5cm, but you need to sow more to allow for those that don't germinate.

■ To sow sparsely, hold the seed packet fairly high above the drill, which should be about 8cm wide. As you move slowly along the drill, tap the packet to release the seeds. Do not do this if it is windy or the seeds will blow all over the garden.

■ So that you are not too heavy-handed when sowing carrot seeds, mix the quantity of seeds required (4g per $10m^2$) with dried coffee grounds. It is easier to scatter this relatively bulky and clearly visible mixture in the drill. It is also said to protect the crops from carrot root fly and other insects.

■ Alternatively, mix the seed with sand and you will also be able to sow the seed more evenly. You will still have to thin the seedlings to give the plants enough space.

Sow carrots with onions and leeks These plants are all attacked by specific flies or moths that are attracted to their host plants by smell. Planting alternate rows of carrots and onions, or leeks, disorientates and discourages these pests.

Mix carrot and radish seeds Sow these crops together and, because radishes germinate much more quickly than carrots, they will mark out the rows and enable you to see where to hoe. You will have harvested the radishes before the carrots need the space to grow into.

■ You can also plant carrots with aromatic herbs, especially coriander, dill and rosemary. These also have the advantage of providing a certain degree of protection against carrot root fly.

Make a barrier against carrot fly The carrot fly, whose maggots do so much damage by burrowing into the roots, finds its host plant by flying just above the surface of the soil. Protect your carrots by erecting a barrier of fine netting or horticultural fleece attached to a frame around one or two rows at a time. The frame should be higher than the plants and can be kept in place with canes.

■ Remove and destroy any infested plants immediately.

■ As the carrot fly lays its eggs in late May, sow plants from mid June to early July to avoid infestation.

■ A strong-smelling substance such as soot or powdered seaweed applied on the soil may also help to deter carrot fly.

Harvesting carrots

Usually, if you try to pull a carrot by the foliage, you'll end up with the leaves in your hand and the root still firmly in the ground. Before pulling, push the carrot gently into the soil – this enlarges the hole, breaks the rootlets that anchor the root in the soil and makes it easier to pull up.

Precision weeding Removing weeds from a row of carrots is an extremely delicate operation. One traditional suggestion is to use a knitting needle.

Forked roots Carrots can be deceptive. Large necks, full of promise, may emerge above the soil but, when it is time to lift them, the carrots revealed by your garden fork are often a disappointment – the root has stopped short after a few centimetres and given rise to new taproots. These are known as forked roots.

■ The fault lies in the soil. Forked roots are caused by a deeper, compacted layer of soil (the result of working the soil to the same depth each year), by poorly structured soil with hard lumps, or by the presence of partially rotted manure. They can also be caused by insects and other disease-causing parasites. Dig the soil deeper and more thoroughly next year.

Deterring rabbits Some gardeners have had success in deterring rabbits with the old-fashioned practice of poking matchsticks, head down, into the soil near each carrot.

Protecting root crops with a clamp In the past, carrots, potatoes, turnips, parsnips and beetroot were stored over winter in an outdoor 'clamp' – a sort of straw hut – to protect them from the weather. Vegetables had to be retrieved for eating with care and any gaps closed to avoid unbalancing the heap. It was also recommended that the heap was opened only at noon so that the sun's rays would prevent that part of the heap from being frozen.

■ Alfred Smith, a Victorian market gardener, wrote about the traditional construction of a clamp. It was placed in a high but sheltered place where the ground was well drained. A shallow pit 30cm deep and 1.5m² was dug in the soil and covered with a thick layer of straw. The vegetables were then arranged on the bed in a ridged heap 90–120cm high.

Thin carrot seedlings under horticultural fleece where they are protected from the low-flying pest, carrot root fly.

To fertilise or not?

Root crops don't have the same nutritional needs as salad greens or tomatoes. Although they need nitrogen to promote a good yield and early cropping, too much nitrogen will produce watery roots that don't store well. In addition, they need phosphorous and potassium to promote the build-up of reserves in the root and produce good-quality vegetables, as well as the magnesium and trace elements essential for human health.

If you haven't been able to prepare the soil in advance, all these elements are available in commercial organic fertilisers made from natural products. Fertilisers for root vegetables should contain less phosphorous than nitrogen and a lot more potassium – check the NPK (nitrogen, phosphorous, potassium) formula on the packaging. Also check that they contain reasonable quantities of magnesium.

Storing carrots and other root vegetables in sand

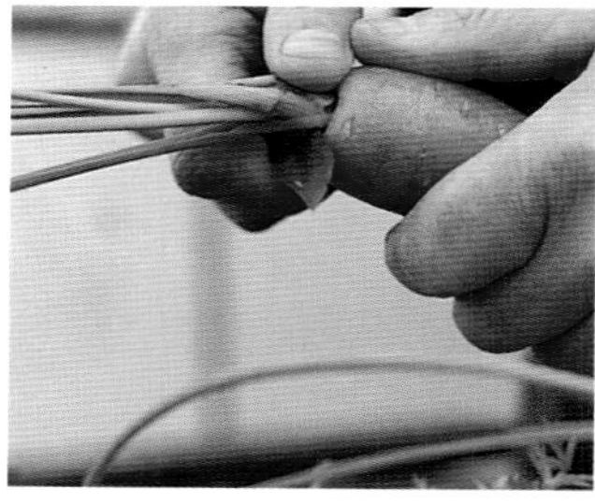

1 After harvesting the carrots, wash off the dirt and cut off the feathery tops.

2 Store carrots in single layers in boxes, alternating with layers of damp sand.

3 Cover them with a final layer of sand and store in a cool, frost-free shed.

Another layer of straw was placed over the vegetables, to a depth of at least 30cm, followed by a 30cm layer of the soil dug from the pit. Funnels of straw were then made in the sides or at the top for ventilation, to prevent rotting.

■ Carrots were piled up to form a cone shape, their top ends facing outwards, and covered in sand only, not straw or earth. Potatoes were piled this way too.

Drying out is essential Once you have pulled or lifted your carrots, leave them on the surface of the soil for a day or two to ensure that they keep well. This process, known as 'drying out', firms up the skins and is essential before they are stored in a clamp or in a cool cellar over winter. When carrots have been lifted, cut off the foliage just above the neck, the point where it joins the root.

Storing carrots in the ground The best way to store main-crop carrots is actually to leave them in the ground over winter. But if the temperature drops very low – below –5°C – they may be damaged by frost. Covering them with a 5cm layer of dead leaves or straw, held in place with a piece of horticultural fleece, will offer a degree of additional protection.

Using crates Line a wooden fruit crate with hessian. Remove excess soil from the carrots, taking care not to damage the roots, but do not wash them. Place a layer of carrots into the box, on a generous layer of insulating material: compost, sand, sawdust or leaf mould. Cover with the insulating material and layer again. Store the crate at a constant temprature of 0–4°C.

Growing radishes

With its colourful skin and white flesh, the radish is one of the spiciest roots in the kitchen garden. The seeds can be sown in succession from February to September to produce a regular harvest of roots. They take only 20–30 days to mature. Sow little and often – into short rows every 14 days – for radishes all summer long.

■ Radishes are a good 'starter plant' for children, who like to see quick results.

Depending on the variety, radishes have white ('Long White Icicle'), red ('Giant of Sicily') and red with white tipped skins ('French Breakfast'). Radishes are a rich source of calcium, iron and vitamin C.

Summer and winter radishes Summer radishes are mainly the globe or round red roots, although some summer radishes are

Fast-growing radishes make an ideal 'catch crop' for planting between main crops of slower maturing vegetables.

Varieties of radishes

Use summer radishes to add colour and bite to salads. In winter, radishes can be cooked to enliven soups and stews.

SUMMER RADISHES

Globe or round 'Sparkler 3', with a white tip, 'Scarlet Globe', 'Cherry Belle' and 'Juliette F1' are reliable, heavy croppers, to add a little decorative zest to summer salads.

Intermediate 'Flamboyant Sabina' and 'Fluo F1' are dependable intermediate varieties. If you want a pure white-skinned radish, grow the intermediate 'White Icicle'.

WINTER RADISHES

Round Winter radishes are usually long, but the Asian radish 'Mantanghong F1', with its magenta flesh and 'Black Spanish Round', with black skin are round. 'Mino Early', has long white succulent roots that make a tasty addition to winter salads, soups and stews. Sow all these in summer for a winter harvest.

Long For strong flavour in a long variety, try 'Rosa 2'. For length and flavour, grow the Japanese radish 'April Cross F1'. It has a crunchy texture and mild flavour and can be left in the ground until you are ready to harvest. It is also known as mooli radish.

more elongated and are known as intermediate radishes. Winter radishes are long and cylindrical in shape.

■ Sow globe or round radishes to a depth of 1cm, while intermediates and winter radishes should be sown a little deeper to 1–2cm. It is important to sow them evenly. If sowing is uneven it results in erratic germination, and early developing seedlings will overshadow later ones.

Protect early sowings Radishes dislike root disturbance and need to be sown in situ. Those sown early, from February through to late spring, will need protection. Use horticultural fleece or a plastic cloche to protect the seedlings from frost.

Sun or shade? Full sun for early and late sowings will mean your radishes do well, but some shade is needed for those sown in midsummer. Radishes prefer well-drained, light soil, but should be well watered to grow succulent and tasty roots.

Getting the best out of radishes For juicy well-shaped radishes, sow them into moist soil and water the growing plants well once the seedlings are established. Thin seedlings to 2cm to avoid the overcrowding that results in lanky plants.

Intercropping and catch cropping As radishes mature so quickly, they are especially useful for intercropping: sowing between other crops while they establish themselves. They are also useful as catch crops in between plantings of main crops. In midsummer, sow radishes as a catch crop or intercrop – they will benefit from being shaded by the other crops, preventing them from bolting in excessive heat.

Easy sowing with treated seed The seedlings of root vegetables usually need to be thinned out so that they have enough room to produce good crops. To avoid this painstaking chore, you need to sow the correct amount and density of seed. But this is not always easy to do, especially with tiny seeds. Fortunately there are now some specially treated seeds available that make accurate sowing much easier. The only drawback is that seed treated in this way is expensive, and there is a limited choice of varieties available.

- **Seed tapes** Seeds are embedded into tapes (below) at even intervals suitable to the variety for regular sowing. All you have to do is make the drill, lay the strip along it and cover it with soil. The days of thinning out will be over for ever.

Seed tapes are biodegradable, so they break down over time when the sowings are watered.

- **Coated seed** Coated or pelleted seeds are surrounded by a protective material that makes them ball-shaped and therefore much easier to handle. This in turn makes it simple to sow them at the correct spacing.

Don't waste any part of your radishes It's a shame to discard the leaves of freshly picked young radishes. Chopped up, they make a delicious garnish or salad ingredient. There is even a variety of radish called 'Rat's Tail', which is grown especially for its hot and spicy seedpods.

Salsify and horseradish

Salsify, the oyster plant Salsify is a biennial root vegetable that produces attractive mauve flowers, which are also edible. The roots are long and brownish, with wrinkled skin and a delicate flavour, often compared with that of oysters or asparagus. It needs an open site and does best on light soils. On heavy clay, it is best to sow into a trench filled with compost or loam. Do not apply manure just before sowing salsify seeds; it is better to sow into a soil that was manured for a previous crop.

- Sow seed in situ in spring for an autumn to winter harvest. The roots keep in the ground, but once harvested they should be eaten promptly, as they shrivel quickly.

Hardy horseradish is grown for its pungent, peppery taproots, which are most usually used in a tangy condiment that goes well with beef.

- Dig and manure the bed in winter. In February, purchase roots, known as thongs, about 25cm long and finger-thick. Plant them vertically so that their tops are 5cm below the surface.
- Lift the roots as required during summer; in winter, lift and store. To save on storage space, borrow a technique from old-time gardeners and lift a root from the winter garden, cut off a piece to use, then replace the root in the soil for another day.

Its long roots are hard to eradicate, so horseradish should be grown as a perennial in a corner where it can be left undisturbed, or dug up each year and replanted in spring.

- Control invasive horseradish plants and coax them into putting down long, straight roots by planting them in galvanised drainage pipes. Sink the pipe up to the rim in a deep hole. Fill with compost-rich soil, insert the horseradish and firm down.

Turnips, swedes and parsnips

Tempting turnips The swollen, fleshy roots, usually white, have a delicate mustard flavour. The tender leaves are also used as a winter green vegetable, and the young shoots may be blanched and eaten. These vegetables should be grown quickly and, except for winter-cropping varieties, may be used as a catch crop.

Choose your varieties There are globular, flattened and long-rooted types of turnip.
- 'Aramis' and 'Model White' are flat-rooted varieties suitable for an early crop.
- For summer crops, the globular 'Tokyo Cross' or 'Snowball' are recommended.
- 'White Globe' is a white, ball-shaped turnip with a deep rim of red at the top.
- For a winter crop, choose the globular 'Golden Ball', which has sweet-tasting yellow flesh. It has hard roots that store well.

A traditional winter crop Turnips were once grown only as winter vegetables, but you can sow fast-maturing types such as 'Purple Top Milan' and 'Snowball' to eat as soon as they reach a suitable size, normally in around 50 days.
- Later-maturing types such as 'Green Globe' can be stored to eat over winter. Crops can be harvested most of the year.

Sow under glass or outdoors Sow early turnips in spring under cover of cloches or in a cool greenhouse. Sow seeds to a depth of 2cm into shallow drills spaced about 25cm apart, then thin to 10cm apart. If you are sowing a main crop it should be sown outdoors.
- For turnips which are to be stored from late autumn through to winter, sow well-spaced in rows 30cm apart, later thinning them to 15cm. Choose varieties suitable to the season and sow in succession every 21 days.
- Turnips grow well in open sites in light, fertile soils that have been well manured. Be careful to bury the manure deeply or the roots may become forked and have an earthy flavour.

Turnips need water Turnips need regular water throughout their growing season or their centres become woody. Spring rainfall usually helps the gardener, but in dry seasons remember to water them well. Lack of moisture later in the season, especially for midsummer-sown turnips, can result in stunted, woody plants, bolting and susceptibility to pests.

Summer turnips are sown from spring onward and the tender roots harvested while still small and juicy.

Growing root vegetables

The chunky swede A winter-hardy crop, swede is grown for its sweet-tasting yellow flesh. It stores well over winter in a clamp (see pages 43-44). Sow seed in spring to a depth of 2cm and thin out to 25cm.

- An open, sunny site in light, well-drained, fertile soil suits this root crop well. It needs regular watering. 'Best of All' and 'Marian' are two reliable varieties.
- The swede has a bad reputation that is totally unjustified, probably a legacy of its overuse in rationing during the Second World War. This hardy and delicious vegetable, which matures in three to four months and is exceptionally trouble-free to grow, deserves its place in our kitchens and vegetable gardens.

Growing parsnips Sunny, open sites are most suitable for parsnips and, although light soil is best for root formation, they will grow on heavy soil too. Prepare the soil the previous autumn for best results.

- **Sow thinly** Sow parsnips in spring in groups of two to four seeds to a depth of 2cm. They are slow to germinate, but when necessary, thin out the seedlings leaving 15–20cm between plants, depending on size of roots required.
- **Avoid drought** During the growing season keep weeds under control and water in dry periods or the roots will split.
- **Harvest after the first frost** Though it is possible to harvest parsnips from the end of summer onwards as you need them, wait if you can until the leaves have been damaged by the first frosts, as this will help to improve their flavour.
- **Leave in the ground** Parsnips can be left in the ground whatever the weather, since it is where they will keep best. Alternatively, they can be stored in crates filled with sand (see page 44).

A rooty parsley Hamburg parsley has roots that look and taste similar to parsnips. They are smaller than parsnip roots, but their foliage stays on the plant throughout winter and can be used as a parsley substitute.

- Hamburg parsley grows well in full sun in light or heavy soils. Sow the seeds in spring and summer to a depth of 2cm and thin plants to 15–20cm.
- Harvest the roots from the end of summer as and when you need them, and store them over winter in the ground or crates of sand.

Sow kohlrabi in pots or a nursery bed in late May or early June. Wait for the soil to warm up before sowing – if you sow when temperatures are below 10°C, the plants will bolt. Kohlrabi is ideal for warming autumn soups and stews, so don't grow it too early in the season or it will develop too rapidly.

Sweetly flavoured and popular as a roast vegetable, parsnips are a reliable winter root that improves as the season progresses.

Kohlrabi

The kohlrabi, or turnip cabbage, is a member of the cabbage family and produces a swollen, edible stem. Although it is not a root vegetable, it has a similar taste and use to the turnip, but is easier to grow. It is also drought-tolerant. So long as the soil is well manured, with a high pH level to lessen the likelihood of club root, kohlrabi will grow equally well in either sandy or heavy soil.

- Sow kohlrabi seeds heavily and thin the plants out rather than transplanting them, as this avoids root damage. Prick them out in their growing positions when the plants have a few leaves, spacing them at 25cm between each plant.
- Harvest as soon as the globes are well formed so that you can enjoy them while they are tender. If left, they become hollow and fibrous, and split open.
- A useful tip: earthing up slightly as the globes begin to form will keep them tender.

Celeriac

Introducing celeriac Long popular on the Continent, celeriac is now increasingly grown in Britain, where it contributes effectively to the traditional self-sufficiency of the winter kitchen garden. It is cultivated for its thick roots which are used as an autumn or winter vegetable. The plant resembles celery, but at ground level it develops a swollen root similar to a turnip.

Celeriac prefers an open sunny site Plant seedlings in fertile soil and water copiously during the growing season. You can leave mature plants in the ground to harvest as you need them, but if temperatures are set to drop to below −10°C, you will need to cover them with a straw mulch or horticultural fleece.

Looking after celeriac
For substantial celeriac with a good rounded shape, give the plants plenty of room, with rows spaced 45cm apart and plants spaced at 30cm. Remove any faded lower leaves to expose the top of the stem and use a knife to cut off any rootlets that develop above the surface of the soil. A good variety to try is 'Snow White'.

Disease-resistant varieties Celeriac is affected by similar diseases and pests to celery. The best solution is to grow disease and pest-resistant varieties such as 'Monarch' or 'President'.

Start celeriac under glass Expect celeriac to have a growing season of at least 26 weeks from sowing, in order to produce good-sized roots. This means it should ideally be started out under glass. Germination can be slow and erratic, so you will need keep an eye on the seed trays. You can either sow into a heated propagator in late winter or early spring, or into a cool greenhouse or cloches in mid spring.

When the seedlings are large enough to prick out, move them on into 7.5cm pots. Harden them off when all danger of frost is past and weather is uniformly warm. Sudden drops in temperature will cause the plants to bolt. Plant out in June or July.

Bulbs and stalks

GIVING A TASTY BOOST TO ANY DISH, ONIONS, SHALLOTS AND GARLIC, AND OTHER FLAVOURSOME BULBS AND STALKS, INCLUDING LEEKS, FENNEL AND CELERY ARE STILL VALUED HIGHLY AS STAPLES OF THE KITCHEN GARDEN AND THE WINTER LARDER.

Onions, shallots and garlic

For best results Onion, shallot and garlic bulbs are fairly easy to grow, and will yield well from year to year if you follow a good rotation system. Allow a gap of two to three years before you grow any other member of the onion family on the same piece of ground. Rotation lessens the likelihood of build-up in the soil of pests and diseases, which means that the plants will be healthy and your harvest from them successful.

Prepare the soil well in advance If you add manure to soil destined for onions too close to planting time, the bulbs may rot off in the ground. And if they do grow, they probably won't be good for keeping. Avoid planting in soil that is high in nitrogen, which promotes leaf growth at the expense of the bulb.

The secret of successful planting

- Onions, shallots and garlic are all planted in the same way. Hold the bulb between your thumb and first two fingers and push it into soil that has been well broken down, so that the point is uppermost and slightly lower than soil level. This will protect the bulbs from birds that might pull them out.
- Sometimes the bulbs are pushed out of the soil by the developing roots a few days after planting. Prevent this by planting each bulb in a narrow but fairly deep hole made with your finger or a dibber. If the bulbs are pushed out of place, they will need to be repostioned, otherwise the roots will grow sideways rather than downwards.
- If you buy onion, shallot and garlic sets for planting from a garden centre, choose plump, healthy sets.

Know your onions Choose onions to suit your requirements.

- **Spring onions** are sown in summer to be harvested and used fresh up to the following spring. They are left in the ground and picked as needed for use in salads.
- **Globe onions** are harvested in late summer and stored to keep through winter.
- **To grow small white onions** for pickling, sow 'Pompei' and 'Paris Silverskin' densely from February to May. They will be ready to harvest and then pickle in summer.

Planting onions Either sow onion seed in January in the greenhouse or plant onion sets (small onion bulbs) in the ground in early spring once the soil has warmed up. Heat-treated onion sets are less likely to bolt and run to seed in hot dry conditions.

Planting onion sets

1 Plant onion sets 1-3cm deep and 10-15cm apart in rows 25cm apart

2 If mice are a problem, start onion sets in pots to plant out once they are bigger.

■ For large onions, sow early or buy onion sets in February or March. Planted at a depth of 3cm and at intervals of 10–15cm, they will be ready to harvest several weeks earlier than onion seeds sown at the same time, and the bulbs will be much bigger.

Onions can be lifted as soon as the tops have died down. Ease them out of the ground using a fork so as not to damage the roots.

In early spring, inspect stored onions and garlic and dispose of any that show signs of rot and mould. Quickly use any that are shooting.

Tasty onions and garlic

Onions 'Red Barron' is a red globe-shaped onion, 'Sherpa F1' is a golden globe-shaped onion and 'Albion F1' is a white globe onion.
Spring onions 'Ishikura' is a Japanese-type bunching onion, 'White Lisbon' has pearly white to green stems, while 'Deep Purple' and 'North Holland Blood Red' have red stems.
Pickling onions 'SY300' has small brown-skinned round onions, and 'Pompei' is similar, with silver skins. Grown for pickling, they can be used as spring onions before they bulb up.
Shallots 'Golden Gourmet' is a yellow-skinned shallot, 'Longor' is cylindrical in shape and has a good flavour and 'Red Sun' has a reddish skin on a round bulb and stores well in winter.
Garlic 'Elephant Garlic' is the biggest bulb of them all, up to 10cm across, and produces juicy cloves with a mild sweet flavour. 'Giant Wight' has a strong flavour. 'Sultop' has rosy red skins. 'Cristo', a classic French variety, has pink cloves.

When the leaves collapse, onions continue to swell As onions reach the end of their growing cycle, the necks appear to collapse and fold over the bulb, sideways. They also begin to turn yellow and dry off. Ideally they should all do this at the same time, for uniform harvesting. If they are late collapsing, you can give nature a helping hand by gently drawing a rake – prongs upwards – across the onion bed, or fold the necks sideways by hand. Leave the onions in the soil to mature.

Harvest onions, shallots and garlic when the foliage has all turned yellow, and when the weather is dry and sunny. Don't remove the foliage: when it has dried out completely, the bulbs can be stored in crates in a cool, dry place. Alternatively, you can plait the dead foliage to make a string, or store bulbs in clean old stockings or tights, knotted between each bulb to prevent contact. Hang for the winter.

■ Before harvesting garlic, some gardeners suggest that you tie a knot in the green stems. Deprived of sap, the leaves will dry out more quickly and force the bulbs to swell. But if you do this take care not to break the stems.

Shallots planted in winter are ready to harvest as early as late June if the weather has been warm, dry and sunny.

Secrets of shallots You can sow shallot seed in a greenhouse from March to April, but it is more usual to grow shallots from sets. Plant shallot sets outdoors in early spring when all danger of frost has passed.

Grow your own garlic In autumn or early spring, plant cloves of garlic in the ground, spaced about 10cm apart.

■ When planting garlic, it is best to choose the largest cloves from the outside of the head. The smaller ones from the inside of the bulb tend to be less successful.

■ If you leave two or three heads of garlic in the ground when harvesting, you can use these cloves later as the basis for your new crop. Plant them individually when they begin to produce little green shoots. As they already have roots, they will grow quickly.

Garlic varieties 'Thermidrome', a white garlic is planted in autumn or early winter for summer harvest. If you plant in autumn you will get higher yields. 'Sultop' is a rosy

Plant garlic cloves in autumn to give them the two months of cold weather they need to grow well.

Jumbo garlic cloves can be planted in cellular trays under glass, to plant outdoors once they have sprouted.

red variety for spring planting, to harvest from midsummer. 'Elephant', the biggest garlic of them all is planted in spring.

Preventing rot Garlic is prone to rot in damp soil. Avoid this by planting in spring into light, sandy soil. Some traditional gardeners used to space the rows widely to 30–40cm. In spring, once the cloves start to shoot, use a hoe to clear some of the soil from around the bulbs.

Leeks, fennel and celery: vegetables for blanching

What is blanching? The purpose of blanching is to tenderise and sweeten a plant's edible parts. Plants that are naturally bitter when grown in full light are usually more palatable when light is restricted. Though some modern varieties are 'self-blanching', traditionalists claim they don't have anything like the flavour and texture of the earlier kinds.

Enjoy leeks through the year The varieties of leeks have different harvest times. The hardiest of them will overwinter well in the ground. They are usually sown at the same time, but take longer to mature.

- **Early varieties** These small to medium-sized leeks are not particularly hardy. They usually take five months to mature from sowing to harvest and are ready for use from September to November. Try 'Armor' and 'Swiss Giant-Zermatt'.
- **Midseason varieties** These are not very frost-resistant and are quite slow to mature, taking seven months from sowing to harvest in November to January, but they are larger than the earlies. Try 'Lyon 2-Prizetaker'.
- **Late varieties** These are even slower to mature, taking eight months from sowing to harvest, but are productive and frost-resistant. Good varieties to try are 'Giant Winter 3 – Vernal' or 'Musselburgh'.

Getting your leeks snowy white You need to plant leeks quite deep in the ground if you want them to be really white. Use a hoe to make a furrow 5cm deep in a 30cm deep trench that has been prepared with well-rotted manure. Then plant the young leeks using a dibber pushed into the soil as far as possible. About a month after planting, draw 3–5cm of soil back into the trench around the stems.

- Repeat this process each month until there is a ridge of soil on either side of the stems reaching just below the base of the leaves. Tie corrugated cardboard collars around the stems before earthing up, to keep grit off the leeks.
- When you hoe off weeds, leave the dead weeds in the furrow to cover the leek stems. They will rot down when covered by the soil in the ridge as it is built up, and help to 'blanch' the leeks as they grow.

Get baby leeks from a late sowing All varieties of leeks take a long time to mature. But if you have forgotten to sow them in seedbeds in March, you can still sow short-season but hardy leeks such as 'Swiss Giant-Zermatt' as late as July and they will overwinter for harvest in spring. Remember that these late-sown leeks will not grow to be as large as those sown at the right time.

- Because they grow in winter, you can plant leeks in the spots where summer

Planting out young leeks

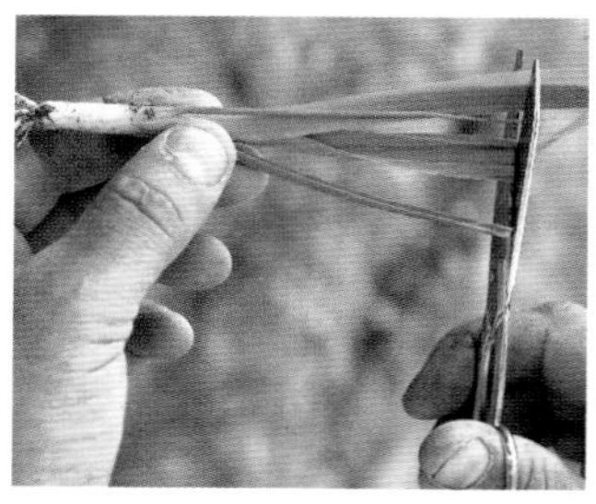

1 Leeks are ready to plant out when they are the size of a pencil. Cut roots back to 1cm and snip off part of the green foliage, reducing the plant to 20cm long.

2 Make a hole with a dibber and plant the leeks so that 10cm – about half their length – is in the ground.

3 Water into the planting hole formed by the dibber. Leave the leeks to find their own level. Check daily while they establish, and replant any the birds pull out.

vegetables such as early peas and salad crops have been harvested.

Beneficial associations There are good and bad companions in the vegetable patch. Carrots, celery, fennel, corn salad, onions and tomatoes can all be grown with leeks – an association that appears to be mutually beneficial. These pairings seem to work because the plants need the same nutrients and will occasionally protect each other against predators.

Faithful standby Leeks are hardy and sit steadfastly in the ground throughout autumn and winter, hardly growing but not deteriorating as long as the temperature stays cold. Leave them in the ground as long as possible and lift as required for cooking.

Florence fennel needs the sun Sow the annual Florence or globe fennel in early summer into a sunny, well-drained soil. Thin seedlings out so that they are spaced 30cm apart. Fennel needs regular watering during its growing period, and if you earth up the soil as the plants begin to fatten up, the resulting bulbs will be whiter and more tender.

■ Choose annual fennel for its squat, bulbous edible stems and sweet, tender leaves, rather than the tall perennial kind, often found in the herb garden.

Harvest leeks when you need them by digging them up with a garden fork.

Fennel can be a difficult neighbour Probably because of its powerful aroma, fennel can be very aggressive when grown next to a number of other vegetables. Only leeks and celery seem to be able to live in the same vicinity.

Fit for the harvest Fennel will be ready to harvest in early to late autumn. Cut the bulb off the stem at ground level, and if you are lucky some flavoursome shoots may regrow from the stump. If you notice that the bulb is beginning to elongate, you must harvest it at once. This is a sign of bolting, which means that the plants will go to seed and the edible parts will become too tough to eat. There are a number of bolt-resistant varieties including 'Argo', 'Amigo F1' and 'Zefa Fino'. If you use these varieties you can sow fennel seed earlier, in the late spring.

Easy-to-grow celery A delicious stem, celery needs blanching to give it its best flavour, though you can also find self-blanching or green celery. It needs a sunny site and a well-prepared loam soil.

For an early start sow into modules in a propagator in a greenhouse. Transplant seedlings sown in the propagator in spring and early summer. If you have sown self-blanching celery, space it 25cm apart. Otherwise trenching varieties need 20–25cm spacing between the plants.

Blanching celery Once the stems are growing well you need to earth the plants up, or enclose each plant with a tube of cardboard. This keeps the stems clean and blanches them.

- Varieties that self blanch include 'Lathom Self-Blanching', 'Greensleeves' and 'Golden Self-Blanching'. They are ready for harvest from late summer to autumn. Sow under cover in early February and transplant in the garden from May onwards.

Fennel in history

A Mediterranean native, fennel was brought to Britain by the Romans. It is mentioned in early Anglo-Saxon herbals and was regarded as one of the nine sacred herbs, said to guard against unseen evil and to restore the eyesight. Chaucer refers to fennel; as does Shakespeare, and fennel grows in his birthplace garden.

Earth up Florence fennel once the stem bases begin to swell and protect with cloches to extend the harvesting season.

Self-blanching and green (American) celery grows fast and is harvested from late summer until the first frosts if grown outdoors.

56 Growing potatoes

THERE ARE TWO TYPES OF POTATO: EARLIES AND MAINCROP. EARLIES ARE PLANTED IN EARLY SPRING AND NEED ONLY 14-15 WEEKS IN THE GROUND TO PRODUCE TENDER 'NEW' POTATOES. MAINCROP POTATOES HAVE A LONGER GROWING SEASON, ABOUT 20 WEEKS AND NEED MORE SPACE, BUT PRODUCE HEAVIER YIELDS AND STORE WELL.

Grow potatoes all year

Potatoes for planting You can always replant small potatoes from last year's crop, but there is no guarantee they'll be disease-free – they may have been contaminated by a virus or be carrying blight spores. A more reliable option is to buy seed potatoes that are certified as disease-free – look for this on the label of the net in which they are sold.

Growing early potatoes Plant earlies into trenches in full sun in well-drained, well-manured soil in early spring. They will be ready for harvest in late June, but you will need to protect them with a cloche or a layer of horticultural fleece. In the north of England plant them in late spring.

■ Plant your potatoes to a full spade's depth: at least 30cm.

Chitting potatoes Sprouts or 'chits' (see picture, left) produce the new potato plants. After you buy your seed potatoes, place them in a box or tray in a light and frost-free room to chit them. The sprouts should be short and firm. Several sprouts may develop on each tuber, though some gardeners suggest you remove all but three.

■ Try sprouting seed potatoes in an old egg carton. Set them with the fattest end up, as this end produces the best sprouts.

Beware of late frosts Young potatoes can still be destroyed by late frosts up until May, especially on clear nights. Hoe and earth up potatoes in their trench if there is any danger of frost. If they are in leaf, you will need to cover the leaves with the soil as well. You may also need an additional protective covering such as horticultural fleece.

Planting early potatoes

Method 1 When each chitted potato has formed four or five shoots 2–3cm long, dig a trench 10cm deep and place them in it, rose end up, and 25–30cm apart; fill in with soil.

Method 2 Plant the chitted tubers in individual holes, using a trowel, at the same depth and distance, in rows 40–50cm apart. Fill in each hole with soil.

Natural die-back of foliage Potatoes come into flower as the tubers ripen. Soon after, the foliage turns yellow and falls onto the soil. This is natural, and should be left until you are ready to harvest the tubers from the ground. You will probably harvest earlies well before the leaves have turned brown.

Earthing up potatoes

1 Plant potatoes to a spade's depth of 30cm, leaving 50cm between plants in all directions. Cover the tubers.

2 When the foliage appears, heap earth around the base of the plant so it hides the stems and forms a mound from which the leaves emerge.

3 Continue to 'earth up' along the entire row. This enables the tubers to form in a compact cluster and protects them from early season frosts.

Harvesting potatoes

Lift maincrop potatoes in fine weather and leave on top of the soil for 24 hours to harden the skins. If you have to harvest in rainy conditions keep them in a dark, warm, well-ventilated place and leave for a few days. This will let them to dry out and lose some of their water content. Don't store any that are damaged or blemished.

The potato hook or Canterbury hoe, with two long, slightly curved prongs is the best tool for lifting potatoes. Stand at right angles to the row and sink the prongs beneath each plant with a single blow. Then all you have to do is pull on the handle of the hoe and any stems above the surface of the soil.

Safe storage Transfer your potato harvest to a basement, shed or storeroom that is frost-free and dark. Potatoes must not be exposed to light as they will turn green and build up a bitter and toxic alkaloid known as solanine. Store in wooden crates or sacks. Avoid plastic, which will make potatoes sweat and rot.

Different varieties of potatoes

It is useful to know if a potato variety is 'first early' (three months from planting to harvest), 'maincrop' (four months) or 'second early' (between the two). Firm or waxy potatoes (A) are boiled in their jackets, sliced in salads and sautéed. Tender and floury potatoes (B) are ideal for baking, puréeing, mashing and adding to soups and stews. You can make good chips with any type of potato.

Consider how disease-resistant your chosen variety is, and how you will treat your crop if it needs protection.

* Poor ** Average *** Fairly good

VARIETIES	EARLY/ MAINCROP	CULINARY GROUP	DISEASE-RESISTANCE
'Amandine'	First early	A, B	***
'Amour'	Maincrop	A, B	***
'Arran Pilot'	First early	A, B	***
'Belle de Fontenay'	First early	A	*
'British Queen'	Second early	B	**
'Désirée'	Maincrop	A, B	**
'Pink Fir Apple'	Maincrop	A	**
'International Kidney'	Maincrop	A	**
'Kestrel'	Second early	B	***
'King Edward'	Maincrop	A, B	**
'Nadine'	Second early	A, B	***
'Pentland Javelin'	First early	A	***
'Ratte'	Second early	A	*
'Roseval'	Maincrop	A	*
'Vilja'	Second early	A, B	***
'Winston'	First early	A, B	***

Growing your own herbs

IMAGINE AN OLD-FASHIONED GARDEN AND YOU MAY PICTURE A SUNNY BED OF HERBS. GROWING THESE AROMATIC PLANTS – HIGHLY PRIZED FOR THEIR CULINARY AND MEDICINAL QUALITIES – HAS A LONG AND ANCIENT TRADITION WE STILL VALUE TODAY. FORTUNATELY, HERBS ARE VERY EASY TO GROW AND POSITIVELY THRIVE ON POOR, DRY SOILS.

Herbs to sow annually

Dill and carrots make good partners Dill is an aromatic annual that is ideal for sowing among carrots (one or two seeds per metre along a row) as it is said to act as a deterrent to the carrot fly.

■ Its aromatic summer leaves flavour omelettes and fish dishes, especially salmon.

Varieties of basil A highly aromatic herb, basil is grown as a half-hardy annual in cool temperate climates. Most people know the large, floppy foliage of 'lettuce-leaf' basil but there are many other varieties to choose from, such as 'Dark Opal' with purple leaves. Basil is useful in salads as well as a flavouring for cooked dishes.

■ If you get the chance, try planting bush basil, with masses of tiny leaves, 'cinnamon' basil, 'anise' basil and lemon basil.

■ Cut out the growing tip of the basil shoot to encourage the plant to bush out.

Sowing basil in a greenhouse Basil is best sown into seed trays or modules in a greenhouse and then hardened off and transplanted when all danger of frost is past. Seeds need a minimum temperature of 20°C. Water sparingly by standing the seed tray in a bath of water so it will draw moisture in, rather than watering from overhead. When the seedlings are growing well, prick them out into larger pots and grow on until it is safe to plant them outside. In warmer climates where night temperatures do not fall below 13°C you can sow direct into the soil. Again, water plants from the base.

Aniseed is a half-hardy annual Sow the plants directly into the soil when all danger of frost is past. Aniseed needs full sun, some shelter and well-drained soil to thrive. By late summer the seeds are ready to harvest and use in the kitchen.

■ The ripe seed is ideal for flavouring cakes and pastries, and the feathery foliage, which you can cut all through the growing season, is also delicious in salads.

Try out a variety of different herbs in their pots before planting up a large container or window box for kitchen use.

Herbs for the pot

If you have little space in your garden many herbs will grow well in containers. Plants that thrive in confined spaces include basil, bay (in a large pot), chervil, chives, dill, lavender, lemon balm, lemon verbena, marjoram, mint, parsley, rocket, rosemary, sage, tarragon, thyme and winter savory.

The star-shaped flowers of borage are sky-blue, and are highly ornamental in the garden and at the table. The grey-green leaves are thick and hairy. However, borage is best known as a medicinal plant and will also attract bees for honey production.
■ Once you've introduced it into your garden, it will be there for ever, as it self-seeds copiously. If it appears where you don't want it, treat it as a weed and pull it up.

Perennial onions to sow Welsh onions are useful all year round. A small clump will bulk up over time to form a large one. Lift and divide the clumps in spring to make more plants. Alternatively, if you leave a few flower heads to set seed, the seeds are easy to gather and sow to make more plants.

Dividing basil

1 Acclimatise the plant by standing the pot in its plastic sleeve in a cool, well-lit place. Turn down the sleeve a little each day. Water gently if dry.

2 When you can remove the plastic sleeve without the plants drooping, gently tap out the contents of the pot.

3 Slice the rootball into several segments. Pot up each piece in a 10cm pot of soil-based compost, water gently and stand in a lightly shaded place.

4 Once the plants recover and stand upright, you can grow and pot them on in the usual way.

Coriander – leaves or seeds? For best results sow coriander direct into its growing site when all danger of frost is past. If you are growing it primarily for seed, give the plants adequate space and plant them early, in May or June. If the aromatic foliage is of more interest, sow seed later, in July. There are also some varieties that are specially developed for their foliage. Grow coriander in partial shade for better leaf production.

The subtle taste of chervil With aniseed-flavoured feathery foliage, chervil is a hardy biennial, although it is usually treated as an annual. Sow seed in trays or pots in a cool greenhouse in early spring or outdoors in late spring. Where it is sown directly into the ground, thin seedlings to 25cm. Chervil seedlings are delicate and need careful handling when planting.
■ Grow them in partial shade as otherwise the plants will bolt and run to seed.

Tasty cumin and caraway seeds Cumin and caraway produce masses of seeds that lend a distinctive taste to spicy, fragrant dishes.
■ Cumin is a tender annual. Sow it in a heated propagator in a greenhouse in spring. Transplant into well-drained soil in a sheltered, sunny site.

■ Caraway is a hardy biennial. Sow seed into rich loamy soil in spring. It grows well in full sun. You can also sow it in early autumn to overwinter.

Chives are hardy perennials, but they die down in winter so are often sown annually. Sow seed early in trays of modular cells in a greenhouse in spring. Harden off and plant out in late spring or early summer, in well-drained soil in full sun. Alternatively, you can buy small plants from garden centres or herb specialists. Their pink flowers look attractive in the front of a border.

■ In mild winters the new shoots may develop early. If this happens, cover them with a cloche or horticultural fleece to protect them and encourage the shoots over winter.

■ To ensure the plants are vigorous and healthy, divide the clump into smaller sections every two to three years, in early spring. Plant the smaller sections 25–30cm apart in rows.

If you divide chives in summer, cut them back to 5cm above ground level.

Tarragon thrives in well-drained, frost-free and sunny sites. It needs protection at its crown from excessive winter wet. Plant it out into the ground in spring when all danger of frost is past, or grow it in a large container. Although it has small yellow flowers, they rarely appear, nor does it set seed in cool climates. It is best to propagate by taking cuttings in spring or early summer.

Winter and summer savory Summer savory is an annual that is often grown with broad beans. The beans are delicious cooked with summer savory and the plant is said to deter aphids from attacking the bean plants. Winter savory can be used in a similar way. It is a hardy perennial and has a good flavour in winter.

Use sorrel like spinach Sorrel is a hardy perennial whose large leaves can be lightly cooked and used in the same way as spinach. The lemony young leaves can also be added raw to salads or as a tasty addition to savoury white sauces. Common sorrel *Rumex acetosa* may be too invasive so you may prefer to grow the ground-covering buckler leaf sorrel (*R. scutatus*), with silvery green shield-shaped leaves. Sorrel grows well in partial shade in well-drained soil.

Popular parsley Iron-rich parsley is a must in any vegetable garden. There are many varieties of curly and flat-leaf parsley.

■ **Flat-leaf parsley** has the most flavour. A good one to try is the variety 'Giant Italian'.

■ **Curly-leaf parsley**, such as 'Moss Curled', is less aromatic than flat-leaf parsley but tasty, with a crunchy texture.

■ **Sow seed into trays** in the greenhouse in spring or in the ground when the soil has warmed up. It takes a while to germinate, but the process of germination is not difficult.

Keeping parsley to use later Parsley stores and freezes well. To keep it for a few days without freezing, wash and place in the refrigerator in an airtight box. To freeze parsley, wash it, pat dry with kitchen towel and put it whole in plastic bags in the freezer. When using frozen parsley, crumble it into the dish or pot before it thaws out.

Running to seed Parsley is a biennial, and in its second year it sends up flowering stems and produces seed. To make sure you have parsley for cutting, sow it in succession every year. When the plants go to seed, it is best to dig them up and use the space for other plants.

Shade-happy herbs

Sweet cicely A large plant with feathery, fern-like foliage, this stately herb grows to a height of over a metre. It is hardy and, once established, will thrive in most conditions. The freshly picked leaves with their lovely aniseed aroma and slightly sweet taste are ideal for flavouring and sweetening desserts. The seeds are also tasty and were once used to freshen and sweeten breath. They were also used as sweets in Tudor times, hence the name, sweet cicely.

Scented lemon balm Although it smells of lemon, lemon balm is botanically close to mint and its leaves have a soothing effect when rubbed on insect bites or nettle stings. It is also used to flavour sauces for chicken and fish and in herbal teas.

■ Lemon balm is a perennial that makes a strong clump in cool, damp soil and can be invasive. Plant a root fragment or a small pot plant. It will seed itself readily.

■ If you have planted the variegated form and then allowed it to seed, only green-leaved plants will appear, as it does not come true from seed.

Flavoursome lovage This unusual hardy perennial has a strong flavour, similar to celery. Lovage grows best in partial shade or sun in well-drained soil and spreads to form large clumps. Top-dress with well-rotted compost in autumn.

Architectural angelica This giant herb is a biennial and grows to several metres. The stems of second-year plants are used in confectionery and baking. Macerate a few pieces of angelica in white wine to make a delicious aromatic wine cup, or use it to flavour cakes and cooked fruit. Angelica produces huge amounts of seed, which self-seed copiously if you leave it all on the plant.

■ Once angelica has set seed, the plant dies and you need to remove old plants. You can hoe off any unwanted plants in spring, leaving a few to develop.

Dividing lemon balm

1 Cut back old top growth close to the ground, then ease out the clump by inserting a digging fork all round the outside and levering it upwards.

2 Use a spade to chop the clump into smaller segments. You may find it easier to split very large clumps in situ and then fork up the segments.

3 Replant only the young outer sections in fresh soil, then firm. Water in dry weather.

Top tips for mint

There are many species and varieties of mint. Low-growing types, such as Corsican mint, are best grown as ground cover rather than for culinary uses. Here are a few of the most popular and best-known varieties.

■ **Spearmint** A mild flavoured mint, this is used to flavour cucumber, yoghurt and tabbouleh, and to make mint tea.

■ **Peppermint or black peppermint** More strongly flavoured than other varieties, peppermint is used to make infusions.

■ **Eau-de-cologne mint** A mint with green, purple-veined foliage, it is highly prized for culinary use.

■ **Pennyroyal mint** This strongly scented wild mint has medicinal properties.

■ **Bowles mint** This is the best mint for making a strong-flavoured mint sauce.

Mint is one of the herbs that can be potted up in autumn to be used during winter.

Spicy horseradish A perennial plant that produces large, elongated leaves and a head of white flowers in summer, horseradish is grown for its white roots, high in vitamin C, calcium and magnesium.

■ The variegated form of horseradish is particularly decorative. Horseradish spreads from root cuttings, so when you dig it out, take care not to leave behind pieces of root.

Old-fashioned horseradish fungicide Gardeners used to steep chopped horseradish leaves in water, then filter the liquid and use it to spray fruit trees for the brown rot that attacks them. It was thought that if it was caught early enough, this spray would help to combat the fungus.

Keep mint in check Mint has a vigorous, invasive habit, spreading by means of creeping underground stems. To prevent it from taking over, plant in a large pot with drainage holes. If the pot does not have drainage holes the mint will become waterlogged and rot. Sink the pot into the ground so that its rim is just above the surface of the soil. Check the rim of the pot occasionally and cut off escaping runners.

Bronze fennel can be cut down in autumn. Or you could leave the stems to be frost-enhanced.

Keep flies out A sprig or two of mint in a glass of water is said to be a good way to keep flies out of a room. You will find that the mint roots very quickly in water and in no time you will have extra plants to give to your friends.

Making a thyme tower

1 Spread a layer of gravel, 5cm deep, in the base of the pot. In the centre stand a length of piping with holes set every 10cm. Add a handful of gravel to keep the pipe in place.

2 Fill around the gravel with soil-based compost up to the level of the first planting pocket. Set a thyme plant in position. Add compost up to the level of the next planting hole.

3 Continue adding compost and planting thymes in the pockets. Fill to just below the pot rim. Finish by planting two or three thymes on top.

4 Use a watering can to fill the pipe with water, which will percolate through to all layers. The picture shows the tower after a few months growth.

Sun-loving perennials

True and false chamomile Chamomile is an evergreen perennial herb. Apart from the common or Roman chamomile used as sweet-smelling lawns, there is German chamomile, which has medicinal properties. Feverfew is also regarded as a chamomile, and it is said to be effective in treating migraines and headaches. It has pale green, sometimes golden, foliage and lots of tiny white flower heads with yellow centres. Chamomile also has a strongly aromatic foliage and its flowers are thought to be beneficial in deterring insect pests from invading other garden plants.

Fennel for the long term The common fennel is another one of those plants that, once established in your garden, will stay there for ever. Although it is a short-lived perennial, fennel produces so much seed that it ensures its survival in most garden conditions. It thrives in full sun, in well-drained soil, and reaches 1.5m or more. For variety, grow the bronze-leaf form (opposite) in the ornamental flower garden.

■ Fennel can be used cooked or raw: its aniseed flavour goes well with fish. Both the leaves and the bulb are useful in the kitchen.

■ As fennel comes from the Mediterranean region, a cold British summer may cause it to run to seed before the bulb has developed properly. To avoid this, grow a bolt-resistant variety, such as 'Zefo Fino'.

Marjoram or oregano? Marjoram is a hardy perennial grown for its aromatic foliage, while sweet marjoram, also known as oregano, is a half-hardy perennial shrub.

■ Marjoram thrives in full sun and well-drained soil. To encourage new leaf growth,

cut back the stems after flowering. Divide established plants in autumn or spring.
■ Sweet marjoram is usually grown in cool temperate climates as an annual. Sow seed in a heated propagator in spring and transplant into the garden in early summer. It grows best in well-drained soil with plenty of added grit.

Growing bay A tree prized for the flavour of its evergreen leaves, bay laurel grows well in the ground and in containers and is often clipped into topiary shapes. Although it is fairly slow-growing, in the ground it can grow to be a large tree of up to 15m. If you don't have space for such a large plant, cut it back, but wait until all danger of frost is past.
■ Move bay grown in tubs into larger pots annually. Protect the pot against frost, which damages the roots.
■ The golden form (*Laurus nobilis* 'Aurea') looks good grown in combination with the green form.

Satisfying sage Forming a shrubby plant in the garden, sage is one of the best-known culinary herbs. There are several varieties with different shaped, coloured and aromatic evergreen foliage.
■ Purple sage (*Salvia officinalis* Purpurascens Group) looks particularly attractive in the flower border.
■ Narrow-leaf sage (*S. lavandulifolia*) has narrow leaves and strong blue flowers.
■ Harvest the leaves for cooking just before the plant flowers, when they are at their most fragrant.
■ Although sage is usually grown for its foliage, its flowers are very attractive and can be used to perfume drawers. Cut back sage plants after flowering to encourage a compact shape.

Propagating sage Although you can increase your stock of sage plants by taking cuttings in the usual way, you can also use a traditional layering technique. In April, fix a trailing stem into the soil and cover it with soil. Wait until late summer for the new plant to root and then cut it free.

Choosing a suitable thyme This native of the Mediterranean scrubland is one of the most versatile herbs in both the garden and the kitchen. Most thymes are hardy perennials, but thrive in full sun in light, well-drained soil.
■ There are many different thymes to choose from, boasting different leaf and flower colours and aromas. Some grow as woody small shrubs, such as the lemon-scented thyme (*Thymus* × *citriodorus* 'Silver Queen'), caraway-scented (*T. herba-barona*) and common thyme (*T. vulgaris*). Other thymes are spreading, mat-forming plants that flower at ground level, such as *T. serpyllum*, with small pinky-mauve flowers, and *T.* var. *coccineus*.
■ Use upright varieties, such as *T.* × *citriodorus*, as small edging plants for formal borders or a herb garden. For a decorative effect, plant mat-forming varieties in cracks in paving and paths, or to tumble over rockeries.
■ Give shrubby thymes a light trim after flowering, to encourage it to grow in a bushy, compact shape.
■ As well as pleasantly scenting the garden, thyme can be used throughout the year in salads and in savoury cooked dishes.

Easy thyme cuttings Simply cut a sprig or two from the mature plant, remove the lower leaves from each stem, and plant so that two-thirds of the stem is in the soil. Water well and the cutting should root in three to four weeks.

Hyssop, an underrated herb Hyssop was highly prized by our ancestors and is mentioned in the Bible. In the 17th century, it was used to dress wounds. Today, it tends to be widely – and unjustly – ignored.

Its flowers attract bees and butterflies to the garden and the bitter, minty taste of its leaves is ideal for making infusions and flavouring dishes.

■ Hyssop is a hardy herbaceous perennial native to the Mediterranean mountains, where it thrives in arid, stony soil. It is fully hardy in this country, as long as it is kept in full sun on well-drained soil. Its needs are similar to those of lavender, catmint and rosemary, and it grows well with them.

■ Grow hyssop from seed sown in autumn or from softwood cuttings in summer and cut it back annually to prevent it becoming too woody.

Rosemary shapes up Rosemary is an evergreen shrub native to Mediterranean scrubland. It responds well to shaping into sculptural shapes including pyramids, cones, balls and spirals. Trim your rosemary often and cut it back in spring, removing any damaged or dead branches. Do not let the plants get leggy.

■ Rosemary grows best in full sun, in very well-drained soil. It will produce small flowers in spring and summer. Rosemary does need shelter from harsh winds and will not tolerate winter wet at its roots. 'Miss Jessopp's Upright' is an old favourite with pretty blue flowers in late spring and autumn. It is also useful as an attractive hedging plant.

Taking rosemary cuttings

1 In spring, cut young shoots about 15–20cm long. Remove the lower leaves.

2 Plant the shoots in trays filled with a multi-purpose compost with added grit.

3 Water sparingly. After four to six weeks check if roots have developed. Plant out in situ the following spring.

Lemon verbena needs winter protection in cool temperate climates, so if you grow it outdoors in containers, you will need to bring it into a frost-free greenhouse in winter. Water well during summer and cut back the stems just as the plant begins to flower. Before you bring it indoors in autumn, it should be cut back again. Water sparingly in winter.

■ If you want to grow lemon verbena outside, plant it against a south or west-facing wall or grow it from softwood cuttings, taken each summer.

Dropping a rosemary

1 Dig up the leggy plant in late winter or early spring and excavate the hole 30cm deeper than it was.

2 Replant in the same hole, spreading out the branches. Return the soil to cover the centre of the plant and the bare portions of the branches.

3 Keep moist in dry weather and transplant any rooted layers in autumn, or leave them to form a wider clump.

Pests and diseases

IF YOU FOLLOW MAINLY TRADITIONAL ORGANIC GROWING TECHNIQUES, YOU SHOULD PRODUCE STRONG, HEALTHY CROPS WHICH ARE RESISTANT TO MOST PESTS AND DISEASES. IF YOUR CROPS DO GET INFECTED, TRY TO USE NATURAL REMEDIES WHERE POSSIBLE.

Leafy vegetables

BLACKFLY AND GREENFLY

These aphids collect in colonies on stems and flower heads of most leafy vegetables. Companion planting can help combat them: chervil, marigolds, nasturtiums and savory are all reckoned to be effective deterrents.

CABBAGE MOTH

■ **Symptoms** Leaves of infested plants are covered with varying-sized holes made by yellowish brown or green caterpillars. On cabbages, these caterpillars bore into the heart and ruin the edible parts with their excrement.

■ **Plants affected** Brassicas, swedes, turnips.

■ **Treatment** Check brassicas regularly and remove the eggs, laid in groups of 20–100 on the undersides of the leaves, and caterpillars. If larvae are numerous, before they burrow into the heart, spray with *Bacillus thuringiensis*, a bacterium which kills the caterpillars within a few days, or an approved insecticide.

CABBAGE ROOT FLY

■ **Symptoms** The maggots of the cabbage root fly (*Phorbia brassicae*) tunnel into the roots, which become riddled with holes and discoloured. The plant is weakened and its growth retarded, while the leaves wilt in hot weather. Serious attacks can cause plants to die. It is mainly the first generation of maggots that tunnel into the roots, while subsequent generations attack the aerial parts of the plant.

■ **Plants affected** Brassicas.

■ **Treatment** Destroy the larvae by practising crop rotation, and use companion crops such as onions to prevent infestation. As the fly lays its eggs at soil level, placing collars around the stems where they meet the soil can help to prevent the larvae getting to the roots. Feed the plants with liquid nettle manure to strengthen their natural resistance to all types of pests and diseases.

CABBAGE WHITE BUTTERFLY

■ **Symptoms** Leaves are ragged and full of holes, and the heart is riddled with tunnels of the blue-green or greenish yellow caterpillars (*Pieris brassicae*), responsible for the damage. If you do not act quickly, only the veins of the leaves remain. Cabbage white caterpillars are easily recognised by their colour, longitudinal stripes and black markings.

■ **Plants affected** All members of the cabbage family, including broccoli, sprouts.

■ **Treatment** Take action at once, before the caterpillars burrow into the heads of the plants. Use an insecticide containing rotenone (derris), natural pyrethrins or *Bacillus thuringiensis*. Remove and crush any eggs.

CELERY FLY

■ **Symptoms** White maggots of the celery fly or leaf miner (*Eulia heraclei*) tunnel within the leaves, causing brown spots to appear. These maggots later become brown pupae. The leaves shrivel and dry up and, if harvested, the stalks have a bitter, burnt taste.

■ **Plant affected** Celery.

■ **Treatment** Pick off affected leaves and destroy. Spray the foliage with an approved insecticide such as derris or pyrethrins. Liquid feed with nettle manure to strengthen growth.

CHICORY FLY

■ **Symptoms** Small white maggots tunnel within the leaves, and sometimes the leaf stalks, which eventually shrivel and dry up. Damage is caused by the maggots of the chicory fly (*Ophiomyia pinguis*).

■ **Plant affected** Chicory.

■ **Treatment** Pick off affected leaves and destroy them. Spray the foliage with an approved insecticide.

CLUB ROOT

■ **Symptoms** Swollen and deformed roots are caused by a soil-borne fungus (*Plasmodiophora brassicae*), which penetrates the plant and forms swellings. The leaves turn yellow and wilt in sunny weather. Symptoms are similar to those of the gall weevil. The spores that are released by the swellings can remain in the soil for up to ten years before becoming active.

■ **Plants affected** All members of the cabbage family.

■ **Treatment** Crop rotation is essential to prevent the disease recurring year after year. Treat young plants with an approved club root treatment before planting out. Lift and burn any affected plants. Make sure that the land is limed and well drained as the fungus flourishes on very acid soils. Before planting, check that the roots of bought brassicas and related plants are healthy. Improve drainage by deep digging and incorporating plenty of humus into the soil.

CUTWORM

■ **Symptoms** Roots are eaten away, severed or riddled with holes. Leaves turn pale with a papery texture. Perforations appear, revealing green or yellowish brown caterpillars, the larvae of moths including the turnip moth, the heart and dart moth and the yellow underwing. They live in the ground, where they feed on roots, but come to the surface at night to devastate the lower leaves and sever plants at ground level. Plants weaken, wither and soon die.

■ **Plants affected** Artichoke, cabbage, lettuce.

■ **Treatment** Weeds provide a favourable environment for these pests, so weed borders and beds regularly. *Bacillus thuringiensis* is a very effective biological solution, destroying the larvae by stopping them eating. Or, pick off the larvae by hand at night when they are at their most active. Maintaining humidity levels in dry weather also hinders their development. When the pest is active, spray with an approved insecticide. Hoe soil around plants during spring and early summer, picking up and destroying any caterpillars that you see.

DOWNY MILDEW

■ **Symptoms** A pale grey fungus appears on leaves, flowers and young shoots and the plant beneath the mildew yellows. The symptoms worsen under cool, damp conditions.

■ **Plants affected** Artichoke, brassicas, celery, leek, onion, spinach, salad greens.

■ **Treatment** Remove and burn all affected parts, then spray with Bordeaux mixture. Rotate crops, avoid overcrowding when planting and limit humid conditions: in a greenhouse ensure good air circulation and avoid splashing leaves when watering. Getting rid of plant debris and damaged plants helps to reduce the conditions under which this fungal disease can thrive.

GALL WEEVIL

■ **Symptoms** Hollow swellings (or galls) are found on the roots. These are the plant's reaction to being attacked by 4mm long white maggots that can be found in the galls. These are the larvae of the adult weevil (*Ceuthorrhynchus pleurostigma*), which is active from late spring to summer.

■ **Plants affected** All members of the cabbage family.

■ **Treatment** Gall weevils are not a damaging pest on established brassicas. The galls do not interfere with root action and growth remains unaffected. However, seedlings are more susceptible. Treat infected crops with a plant-based insecticide containing rotenone (derris).

LEAF MOSAIC VIRUS

■ **Symptoms** Infected leaves become discoloured with yellow or pale green mottling. The plant becomes stunted and deformed and eventually dies. This virus is spread from infected plants by several species of aphid.

■ **Plants affected** Lettuce. Also beans, cucumber and peas.

■ **Treatment** Lift and burn affected plants to prevent the virus spreading. Spray crops with an approved insecticide to control aphids: the carrier of this disease.

LEEK MOTH

■ **Symptoms** Light brown patches appear on the foliage, which is subsequently pierced by numerous tiny holes. The adult moth (*Acrolepiopsis assectella*) has brown wings marked with white and is active between spring and autumn. This moth is mainly a problem in coastal areas of southern and eastern England.

■ **Plants affected** Chive, leek, onion.

■ **Treatment** Plant carrots and celery near leeks to limit an infestation. In the event of an attack, spray with an organic insecticide containing rotenone (liquid derris) or pyrethrins. Search for the pupae in their net-like cocoons on the leaves and crush them.

MEALY APHID

■ **Symptoms** Attacks by a waxy, greyish greenfly are characterised initially by discoloured leaves. The plant is weakened and dies.
■ **Plants affected** Cabbage, apple, chervil, plum, radish, turnip.
■ **Treatment** Ladybirds are the ideal predators but, in the event of serious attack, spray with an insecticide containing pyrethrins or rotenone. Dig up and destroy old stalks to prevent the infection from spreading.

ONION FLY

■ **Symptoms** Onion bulbs are riddled with tunnels. This weakens and often kills the plant. The pest is a fly, *Hylemya antiqua*. Its maggots burrow into the bulbs, moving from plant to plant and often attacking an entire crop.
■ **Plants affected** Onion, shallot.
■ **Treatment** Practise crop rotation. In the event of an attack, treat with an organic insecticide containing rotenone (derris) or pyrethrins. Lift and burn badly affected plants. Dig over infected land in winter to destroy the maggots. Grow seedlings under fine netting or fleece to prevent the flies from laying their eggs.

RUST

Orange blotches appear on the leaves of chicory, spinach and also leeks. Cabbages are affected by white rust (or white blister), which appears as white fungal masses on the leaves.

SLUG

Slugs attack most vegetables, especially young plants with tender leaves. Do not throw slugs onto the compost heap to get rid of them, instead, place them into polythene bags, tie the top and place in your waste bin.

THRIPS

Tiny winged insects attack mainly leeks, causing silvery mottling on the upper surface of the leaves, while the undersides appear dirty. Use sticky traps to eradicate them from the greenhouse. Frequent watering may also help as thrips prefer dry conditions.

Root vegetables

ALTERNARIA LEAF SPOT

■ **Symptoms** *Alternaria* causes grey or brown circular patches of more or less dead tissue to appear on leaves. The leaves dry up and, in some cases, fungus forms.
■ **Plants affected** Carrot, chicory, potato.
■ **Treatment** Limit the spread by removing and burning affected leaves as soon as possible. Spray infected plants with a fungicide containing mancozeb.

ASPARAGUS BEETLE

■ **Symptoms** The plants lose their foliage as the adult beetles and their larvae eat the leaves and outer bark from the stems. This causes the stems to dry up and turn yellowish brown. The adult beetles are black with six yellow blotches on their wing cases.
■ **Plant affected** Asparagus.
■ **Treatment** At the first sign of an attack, spray both the plants and soil with an approved insecticide and repeat as the directions advise.

BEET LEAF MINER

■ **Symptoms** The leaves become marked with fairly large brown spots. The tiny white grubs of the mangold fly (*Pegomya hyoscyami*) burrow inside the leaves and can cause considerable damage.
■ **Plants affected** Beetroot, spinach.
■ **Treatment** Pick off and destroy affected leaves or squash the larvae. Spray the foliage with an approved insecticide at regular intervals until the pest is cleared.

CARROT FLY

■ **Symptoms** The roots are riddled with narrow tunnels and rusty brown lines appear on the skin. The plant is weakened and may die. The destruction is caused by the creamy yellow grubs of the carrot root fly (*Psila rosae*).
■ **Plants affected** Carrot, celeriac, chicory, parsnips.
■ **Treatment** To prevent infestation, choose resistant varieties and sow carrots in early spring or midsummer. Protect plants with fine netting or fleece and lift and destroy infected plants immediately.

COLORADO BEETLE

■ **Symptoms** Leaves are riddled with holes and, in severe cases, are completely eaten away. The beetle is about 1cm long and lays its eggs on the underside of the leaves. Beetle have black and yellow markings, and larvae are pink with black markings. Both do a huge amount of damage.
■ **Plant affected** Potato.
■ **Treatment** You are legally obliged to destroy these pests,

which can devastate an entire crop if you do not act quickly. This is a notifiable pest; an outbreak must be reported to DEFRA (the Department for the Environment, Food and Rural Affairs), and the crop must be completely destroyed.

EELWORM

■ **Symptoms** The main roots bear either tiny white cysts (potato cyst eelworm) or large yellow or brown swellings (root knot eelworm). The lower leaves turn yellow and wither. The plants are often killed before the end of summer and, so tubers may be very small.

■ **Plants affected** Onion, potato, tomato.

■ **Treatment** Lift and burn affected plants and tubers, and practise crop rotation. African or French marigolds (*Tagetes*) planted near your susceptible crops will help to keep this parasite at bay. Do not grow potatoes, tomatoes or onions in infected soil for at least six years. With potatoes, try resistant varieties, such as 'Pentland Javelin' and 'Maris Piper'.

FLEA BEETLE

Found on seedlings of beetroot, brassicas, radishes, swedes and turnips, they pierce small holes in the leaves, which turn yellow.

FOOT ROT

■ **Symptoms** Leaves turn yellow, wilt and dry up. The base of the stem darkens and softens. The roots may also rot. The disease starts at the base of the stem and works its way up. Greenhouse plants are particularly susceptible.

■ **Plants affected** Beetroot, celeriac, cucumber, melon, tomato.

■ **Treatment** Prevent the disease from spreading by destroying infected plants. Replace the surrounding compost and make sure that you use hygienic cultivation techniques. Use only mains water on young seedlings.

GANGRENE

■ **Symptoms** Brown patches appear on the skin and flesh at the ends of potato tubers and around the eyes and lenticels (small openings). The diseased area enlarges until most of the tuber is decayed and shrunken. The responsible bacterium, *Phoma exigua* var. *foveata*, mainly attacks the blemishes caused by forks when lifting potatoes.

■ **Plant affected** Potato.

■ **Treatment** Plant only undamaged, certified seed tubers. Take care when lifting potatoes and remove damaged tubers. Store only healthy tubers in an airy, frost-free place and discard any that appear to be infected.

RED SPIDER MITE

Tetranychus urticae is a parasitic mite that attacks celeriac, causing mottling of the leaves, which subsequently turn yellow, wither and die. It also attacks courgettes, cucumbers, French and runner beans, marrows, peas and tomatoes. Spraying leaves with water will help as the mites thrive in dry conditions.

SCAB

■ **Symptoms** Flat, raised or concave patches appear on the surface of roots or tubers. Common scab is brown, while powdery scab has corky patches that release a brown powder. Scab is caused by bacteria of the genus *Streptomyces*, which thrive in light, sandy or very chalky soil.

■ **Plant affected** Potato.

■ **Treatment** Use prevention rather than cure. Dig in compost but do not lime the ground before planting potatoes. Practise crop rotation, increase the acidity of chalky soils and grow scab-resistant varieties. Do not grow 'Desirée' as it is susceptible to powdery scab. Make sure you plant only healthy seed.

WHITE BLISTER

■ **Symptoms** Raised white spots with opaque blisters, arranged in concentric circles, appear on the lower leaf surfaces. The affected leaves become puckered, with sunken, slightly yellow pits. White blister usually attacks crops between early summer and late autumn.

■ **Plants affected** Members of the cabbage family, radish, turnip.

■ **Treatment** As there is no effective treatment, if the problem is still fairly contained, simply remove the affected leaves. If plants are severely affected, pull them up and dispose of them. Grow resistant varieties.

WIREWORM

■ **Symptoms** Roots and tubers are riddled with narrow tunnels bored by a thin yellow grub about 2–3cm long. The grubs are the larvae of the click beetle (*Agriotes*, family *Elateridae*), which can live for up to five years before turning into an adult.

A major infestation can destroy an entire crop.

■ **Plants affected** Asparagus, beetroot, carrot, potato and many other vegetables.

■ **Treatment** It is quite easy to pick up the larvae by hand when digging over the soil. Keep land well cultivated to expose any wireworms to the birds. Traps are also effective. Place small pieces of carrot or potato on spikes and bury them in the soil at a depth of about 5cm to lure the grubs. Inspect and replace the traps regularly. Lift your potatoes as soon as they are mature to prevent attack. Wireworms are more of a problem on old pasture land.

Fruiting vegetables

BLACK BEAN APHID (BLACKFLY)

Found on the leaves and stems of beetroot, broad beans in spring, and French and runner beans during July and August, large colonies of these aphids stunt the growth of the host plant.

COLORADO BEETLE

This striped yellow beetle is usually found on potatoes, but also attacks aubergines, peppers and tomatoes

CUTWORM

■ **Symptoms** Stems on small plants are severed by earth-coloured caterpillars that gnaw the outer membranes at soil level.

■ **Plants affected** Carrot, lettuce, potato.

■ **Treatment** At night, remove large caterpillars by hand. Rake through the soil to bring the culprits to the surface for birds to eat. Good cultivation in weed-free plots helps to limit cutworms. Apply the natural-control nematode *Steinernema carpocapsae* onto the soil around the plants to parasitise the caterpillars and destroy them fast.

DIDYMELLA STEM ROT

■ **Symptoms** This disease primarily affects the leaves, but can also attack the stems and fruit of members of the squash and marrow family. Slimy brown patches appear along the edge of the leaves, which turn yellow. Stem tissue dies and the end of the fruit shrivels as it rots from the inside. *Didymella* stem rot is caused by a fungus that also attacks certain ornamental plants such as chrysanthemums, fruit bushes and raspberries.

■ **Plants affected** Cucumber, marrow, melon, squash, tomato.

■ **Treatment** Feed the crop with liquid nettle manure to strengthen growth. Dig up and burn badly affected plants. Do not throw plant remains onto the compost heap. Clear up all crop debris at the end of the season and grow crops on a fresh site each year.

GUMMOSIS

■ **Symptoms** Dark grey, sunken spots covered with olive green mould appear on fruit which splits. Gum oozes from the cracks. Mould develops on the surface of the gum. As the blemishes heal, corky tissue forms around the edges. It is caused by *Cladosporium cucumerinum*, which is active when daytime temperatures reach 18°C after a cool night.

■ **Plants affected** Courgettes, cucumber, marrow, squash, tomato.

■ **Treatment** Destroy all diseased fruit, then raise the temperature and reduce humidity if plants are grown in a greenhouse. Grow resistant cultivars. Spray a copper-based treatment to help to prevent the spread of the disease.

LEAF MOSAIC VIRUS

Cucumbers, marrows and tomatoes are particularly susceptible. Mosaic-like or mottled patches appear on the leaves, which become deformed and reduced in size. Young shoots curl and the whole plant may be stunted and die early. On some plants, flower colour is affected.

PEA AND BEAN WEEVIL

■ **Symptoms** Seeds have small round holes, while the larvae can be seen on the surface of the soil, feeding on leaves. Light brown patches may appear on the seed coat. The weevils belong to the genera *Acanthoscelides* and *Bruchus*, whose larvae bore into the pods, then the seeds. Active while the plant is growing, they also destroy stored vegetables.

■ **Plants affected** Broad bean, French and runner bean, pea.

■ **Treatment** Established plants can usually tolerate weevil damage. Act if weevils are eating young plants: use an approved insecticide or cover with fleece.

ROOT ROT

■ **Symptoms** The roots show signs of rot, the base of the stem changes colour and shrivels, and the plant dies fairly rapidly.

■ **Plants affected** Aubergine, broad, French and runner beans, courgette, cucumber, marrow, pea, squash, pepper, tomato.
■ **Treatment** Dig up and discard infected plants and remove the surrounding soil to prevent the spread of infection. Maintain good hygiene and use only sterilised compost to prevent root rot.

SCLEROTINIA ROT (BROWN ROT)

Affects aubergines, broad beans courgettes, cucumbers, French and runner beans, Jerusalem artichokes, marrows, peas, and sweet peppers. It is characterised by a white cottony mould on the leaves and fruit, which becomes discoloured, turns brown and rots. The stems discolour and are covered in dense fungal growth. Large black sclerotia (fungal resting bodies) are embedded in the fungal growth.

THRIPS

Tiny winged insects cause silvery mottling on the leaves of aubergines, courgettes, cucumbers, marrows, peppers, and tomatoes.

WHITEFLY

Whiteflies frequently attack fruiting vegetables, weakening the plants by sucking their sap.

Pods and cobs

ANTHRACNOSE

A fungal disease that attacks peas, French and runner beans in wet weather. Dark brown cankers form on stems, leaf ribs turn pinky brown and sunken brown spots appear on the pods.

BLACK BEAN APHID (BLACKFLY)

These aphids are particularly attracted to broad and runner beans, so much so that some gardeners grow a few bean plants in flower borders to keep flowers and shrubs free of blackfly.

HALO BLIGHT

■ **Symptoms** Greasy, water-soaked spots appear on the leaves and pods. Those on the leaves become surrounded by a greenish yellow 'halo', while those on the pods exude a pale cream or silvery bacterial ooze. Infected pods discolour and shrivel, and the seeds are contaminated. This blight is caused by the bacterium *Pseudomonas phaseolicola*, which becomes active in wet, windy conditions that turn dry and hot in the flowering season.
■ **Plants affected** French and runner bean, broad bean.
■ **Treatment** Spraying with copper may protect plants from the disease. Lift and destroy diseased plants, practise crop rotation and do not soak seeds before planting.

PEA MOTH

■ **Symptoms** Inside the pods, the greenish yellow, black-headed caterpillars burrow into the seeds. They are about 1–2cm long and are easily detected by their excrement, which remains attached to a silken thread. The pea moth (*Laspeyresia nigricana*) has a wingspan of about 3cm. It is particularly active in hot, dry weather and during summer.
■ **Plant affected** Pea.
■ **Treatment** Treat affected plants with an organic insecticide containing rotenone (derris) or natural pyrethrins, spraying about seven days after the onset of flowering. Kill the adult moths by using a pheromone trap.

RUNNER BEAN RUST

■ **Symptoms** Yellow pustules cover the upper surfaces of the leaves, while yellow blisters distort the underside and eventually affect the pods. These blemishes turn brown, then black. This strain of rust is caused by the *Uromyces appendiculatus* fungus, which develops during hot, wet summers.
■ **Plants affected** French and runner beans.
■ **Treatment** Grow beans in well-manured ground and feed regularly with liquid nettle or comfrey manure. At the first sign of attack, spray with an approved sulphur-based fungicide.

SMUT

■ **Symptoms** Sweetcorn seeds turn black and release a black powder when opened. Brown patches appear on the leaves of leeks. Different genera of fungus are responsible for this disease – *Entyloma*, *Sphacelotheca*, *Ustilago*, *Uroscystis* – and are spread by rain splash or watering.
■ **Plants affected** Sweetcorn, leeks, onions.
■ **Treatment** Lift and burn plants at the first sign of attack. Do not plant the same crop in a place where the previous crop was infected. Fungicides have no effect on smut.

72 Vegetable planner

USE THIS PLANNER TO SEE WHEN TO SOW OR PLANT IN ORDER TO GET A SUCCESSION OF CROPS TO HARVEST THROUGHOUT THE YEAR. MANY CROPS CAN BE STARTED UNDER GLASS OR IN POTS DURING THE WINTER MONTHS AND PLANTED OUT WHEN THE WEATHER IS MORE FAVOURABLE FOR GROWTH.

	JANUARY	FEBRUARY	MARCH
ARTICHOKES (GLOBE)		sow (glass)	
ASPARAGUS			
AUBERGINES			sow (glass)
BEANS			
broad		sow (glass)	sow (glass), plant
French			
runner			
BEETROOT			sow (mild areas)
BROCCOLI	harvest		harvest
BRUSSELS SPROUTS	harvest	harvest	sow
CABBAGES			
Chinese	harvest	harvest	
spring		harvest	harvest
summer			sow
autumn/winter	harvest		
CALABRESE			sow (glass)
CARROTS		sow (mild areas)	sow
CAULIFLOWER			
summer			sow
autumn/winter	harvest	harvest	harvest
CELERIAC		sow (glass)	sow (glass)
CELERY			sow (glass)
CHICORY	harvest forced	harvest forced	sow non-forcing
KALE	harvest	harvest	
LEEKS	harvest		sow
LETTUCES		sow (glass)	sow
MARROWS, COURGETTES			
ONIONS (ENGLISH)			sow, plant sets
PARSNIPS	harvest		sow (mild areas)
PEAS		sow early varieties	sow
PEPPERS			sow (glass)
POTATOES			
early	sprout	sprout, plant	plant
maincrop			sprout
RADISHES		sow	sow
RHUBARB	force, harvest	harvest	harvest outdoor
SPINACH	harvest	harvest	sow
SWEDE	harvest		sow
SWEETCORN			
TOMATOES (OUTDOOR)			sow (glass)
TURNIPS			sow

	APRIL	MAY	JUNE	
	sow, plant out	plant out	harvest	ARTICHOKES (GLOBE)
	plant crowns, harvest	harvest	harvest	ASPARAGUS
	prick out	plant out (mild areas)	plant out	AUBERGINES
				BEANS
	sow, plant	sow, plant	harvest	broad
	sow (glass)	sow, plant	sow, plant out	French
	sow (glass)	sow, plant	sow, plant out	runner
	sow	sow	sow	BEETROOT
	sow, harvest	sow	plant out	BROCCOLI
	sow	plant out		BRUSSELS SPROUTS
				CABBAGES
				Chinese
	harvest			spring
	sow	plant out	plant out	summer
		sow	plant out	autumn/winter
	sow (glass), plant	sow, plant	sow, plant out	CALABRESE
	sow	sow	sow, harvest	CARROTS
				CAULIFLOWER
	sow in pots, plant	sow, plant	plant out	summer
	sow	sow, plant	plant out	autumn/winter
		prick out	plant out	CELERIAC
	sow in pots	prick out, plant	plant out	CELERY
	sow, harvest	sow (forcing)	sow (forcing)	CHICORY
	sow	sow	plant out	KALE
			plant	LEEKS
	sow, plant	sow, plant	sow, harvest	LETTUCES
	sow (glass)	sow (glass), plant	sow, plant out	MARROWS, COURGETTES
	plant out	plant		ONIONS (ENGLISH)
	sow	sow		PARSNIPS
	sow	sow	sow, harvest	PEAS
	prick out	plant out (mild areas)	plant out	PEPPERS
				POTATOES
	earth up	earth up	harvest	early
	plant out	earth up, plant	earth up	maincrop
	sow	sow	sow, harvest	RADISHES
	harvest (non-forcing)			RHUBARB
	sow	sow	harvest	SPINACH
	sow	sow	sow	SWEDE
	sow (glass)	plant out, sow (glass)	plant out, sow	SWEETCORN
	prick out	plant out (mild areas)	plant out	TOMATOES (OUTDOOR)
	sow	sow	sow	TURNIPS

	JULY	AUGUST	SEPTEMBER	
ARTICHOKES (GLOBE)	harvest	harvest		
ASPARAGUS			harvest	
AUBERGINES		harvest		
BEANS				
broad	harvest	harvest	harvest	
French	sow, harvest	harvest	cover, harvest	
runner	harvest	harvest	harvest	
BEETROOT	sow, harvest	harvest	harvest	
BROCCOLI	plant out			
BRUSSELS SPROUTS				
CABBAGES				
Chinese	sow	sow, plant out	cover plants	
spring	sow (cold areas)	sow, plant	plant out, cover	
summer	harvest	harvest	harvest	
autumn/winter	plant out		harvest	
CALABRESE	harvest	harvest	harvest	
CARROTS	sow, harvest	harvest	harvest	
CAULIFLOWER				
summer	harvest	harvest	harvest	
autumn/winter	plant out		harvest	
CELERIAC				
CELERY	harvest	harvest	harvest	
CHICORY		sow		
KALE	plant out			
LEEKS	plant			
LETTUCES	sow, harvest	sow, harvest	harvest	
MARROWS,	harvest courgettes	harvest	harvest	
COURGETTES		harvest	harvest	
ONIONS (ENGLISH)		harvest	harvest	
PARSNIPS			harvest	
PEAS	sow, harvest	harvest	harvest	
PEPPERS			harvest	
POTATOES				
early	harvest	harvest	harvest	
maincrop		harvest	harvest	
RADISHES	sow, harvest	sow, harvest		
RHUBARB				
SPINACH	sow, harvest	sow, harvest	sow, harvest	
SWEDE			harvest	
SWEETCORN	harvest	harvest	harvest	
TOMATOES (OUTDOOR)		harvest	harvest	
TURNIPS	sow, harvest	sow, harvest	harvest	

OCTOBER	NOVEMBER	DECEMBER	
cover			ARTICHOKES (GLOBE)
			ASPARAGUS
			AUBERGINES
			BEANS
	sow under cloche		broad
cover, harvest			French
harvest			runner
harvest or cover			BEETROOT
			BROCCOLI
	harvest	harvest	BRUSSELS SPROUTS
			CABBAGES
harvest or cover	harvest	harvest	Chinese
plant and cover			spring
			summer
harvest	harvest	harvest	autumn/winter
harvest	harvest	harvest	CALABRESE
harvest	harvest or cover	harvest or cover	CARROTS
			CAULIFLOWER
			summer
harvest	harvest	harvest	autumn/winter
harvest			CELERIAC
harvest	force indoors	force indoors	CELERY
			CHICORY
	harvest	harvest	KALE
harvest	harvest	harvest	LEEKS
sow (glass)	sow, harvest, cover		LETTUCES
			MARROWS, COURGETTES
harvest			ONIONS (ENGLISH)
harvest	harvest or cover	harvest	PARSNIPS
			PEAS
			PEPPERS
			POTATOES
			early
harvest	harvest		maincrop
			RADISHES
	force	force indoors	RHUBARB
harvest	harvest or cover	harvest	SPINACH
harvest	harvest or cover	harvest or cover	SWEDE
			SWEETCORN
		sow (glass)	TOMATOES (OUTDOOR)
harvest	harvest or cover	harvest or cover	TURNIPS

the fruit garden

78 Creating a fruit garden

FEW GARDENS NOW HAVE THE LUXURY OF SPACE FOR AN ORCHARD DEVOTED EXCLUSIVELY TO FRUIT TREES, WITH FRUIT BUSHES AND CLIMBERS PLANTED ELSEWHERE. BUT EVEN IF YOU DON'T HAVE MUCH ROOM YOU CAN STILL, WITH CAREFUL PLANNING, HAVE A FRUIT GARDEN THAT WILL TAKE YOU THROUGH THE SEASONS.

Even a tree in a seemingly constrained space can bear a lavish harvest as in this wall-trained pear.

Assessing the site

Local climate is probably the strongest influence on the type of fruit you can grow. Although you can relieve the effects of high rainfall with efficient drainage, and compensate for too little rain by improving the soil and watering, other factors are critical to productivity.

■ **Temperature** Peaches, apricots and figs do well in long, hot summers, while apples, pears, plums, gooseberries and currants need cooler conditions, especially in winter. Late spring frosts can damage buds, flowers and young shoots.

In very mild districts, the only option is to choose fruits that revel in heat. In cold gardens, note where frost lingers and plant elsewhere; never plant at the bottom of a slope, where cold air tends to collect. If you have no choice, plant taller fruit trees and late flowering bush fruit varieties in the cold spots, reserving the warmer sites for smaller, earlier flowering plants.

■ **Wind** Strong winds discourage pollinating insects, injure flowers and cause fruits to drop prematurely. Protect with a windbreak of netting or open-board fencing, a hedge of beech, or a row of trees such as willow. Avoid building a wall or solid fence that will block the wind and cause turbulence.

■ **Sun and shade** Warm-climate crops, like peaches and greengages, and late ripening top, or tree, fruit need the most sunshine, whereas most soft fruits will tolerate some shade for up to half the day. You can train certain fruits on a fence or wall, allowing the fruits to benefit from the reflected warmth of the sun. Avoid deep shade, especially under overhanging trees.

■ **Soil** Most soils are suitable for growing fruit, provided they are well drained. You should dig heavy clay deeply to prevent waterlogging and work plenty of compost or well-rotted manure into light soils to improve water retention.

When to start

Ideally, carry out preparation in summer to early autumn, clearing the weeds first and using weedkiller, if necessary, to get rid of any perennial weeds. In early autumn dig the ground over thoroughly, to allow it several weeks to settle before starting any of your planting.

Planting cordon apples

1 Dig a bed 1m wide and at least a spade blade deep, and add plenty of garden compost or rotted manure. Drive in an 8cm diameter post every 3m along the strip, and staple taut horizontal wires to the posts about 60–75cm apart. Space cordons 60cm apart, marking the position of each with a cane inserted at 45° and tied to the wires.

2 Plant a cordon beside each cane, at the same angle, and attach the main stem to the cane with adjustable tree ties. Either prune now, shortening sideshoots by half, or wait until spring. A low sideshoot has been retained on the first tree to train vertically on an upright cane to fill the empty triangular space.

Pruning and training

Top fruits, such as apples, pears and 'stone fruits' like plums, cherries and peaches, grow naturally into large trees, but you can prune and train most of them to create a more attractive and productive shape that occupies much less space (see also Rootstocks on page 80). Soft fruits that can be pruned and trained into restricted shapes include bushes such as gooseberries and red and white currants.

- **Standards, bushes and pyramids** In most open ground, you can train tree fruits like apples, pears, and cherries as standards with 1.5–2.2m trunks, half-standards with 1–1.5m trunks, bushes with stems up to 1m high and cone-shaped dwarf pyramids, 2.2–2.5m high. Gooseberries and red-currants are grown as bushes, with 15cm stems, or standards with a 1–1.2m stem.
- **Cordons, espaliers and fans** You can train all tree and bush fruits (except blackcurrants) flat against walls and fences, or on wires stretched between posts. The commonest forms are cordons (see box, left), which are upright or angled straight stems with short fruiting sideshoots; these are used for apples, pears, gooseberries and red or white currants. The same fruits are also suitable for growing as espaliers, which have a central trunk with pairs of opposite, horizontal branches.

Fans, which have branches radiating from a short central trunk, are best for plums, cherries, figs, apricots and peaches; they also suit apples, pears and gooseberries. Blackberries and hybrid berries can be grown flat on wires, informally or as neat fans, and thornless varieties on pillars and arches, like a climber.

Preparing the ground

The best way of preparing the ground is to do it in simple stages.

- **Mark out the fruit garden area** with canes and string or a garden line, marking

Rootstocks and fruit tree sizes

Most fruit trees are grafted onto a standardised rootstock which controls the vigour of the tree and reduces its natural size. Some fruits such as apples and, to a lesser degree, pears, are supplied on a range of rootstocks, from vigorous to very dwarfing, whereas only one or two kinds are available for plums, peaches and cherries. To get the most from a limited space, you need to combine a restrictive form of training with an appropriate rootstock. Good catalogues list the rootstocks available, the trained forms they suit, their ultimate sizes and recommended spacing.

approximate planting positions (these depend on fruit type and form).

- **Spray weeds** with a systemic weedkiller such as glyphosate, and leave for three weeks for it to take full effect. Alternatively, fork out perennial weeds.
- **Dig the whole area** – single digging is sufficient for good soil, but double digging is advised for soil that is impoverished or full of weeds, or where drainage is poor.
- **Feed the soil** and improve drainage by digging in garden compost or well-rotted manure, spreading an 8cm layer in each trench as you dig.
- **Leave to settle** for at least a month before lightly forking and levelling the surface prior to planting.
- **If you are making a bed in an old lawn,** skim off the top 5-8cm of turf with a spade and bury this upside down while you are digging. This will improve the soil's texture as well as its holding qualities.

Planting the fruit

Store trees and bushes safely if you can't plant them at once. If they look dry, plunge the roots in a bucket of water for 2-3 hours before planting. Trim back any damaged roots, and shorten very long ones to 30cm.

Planting a bare-rooted tree

- **Mark the planting position** of the tree with a cane, spacing it an adequate distance from any neighbours. Dig a hole large enough to take the roots comfortably when they are spread out, and at a depth that leaves the old soil mark on the stem at ground level.
- **Drive in a vertical stake** 8–10cm off-centre and on the lee side of the tree (the side away from the prevailing wind). The top of the stake should reach a third of the way up the trunk, or up to the first branches in exposed positions.
- **In a bucket,** mix 5 litres of planting mix, using equal parts of well-rotted manure and garden compost or leaf mould, plus 140g each of seaweed meal and bone meal. Fork this into the excavated topsoil.

Bare-rooted trees should be planted as soon as they are delivered but if soil or weather conditions are unsuitable, make sure the roots stay covered to prevent them from drying out.

■ **Hold the tree upright** in its hole, spread a few trowels of the planting mix over the roots, and gently shake the tree up and down so that the mix settles. Repeat and firm the mix lightly with your foot.
■ **Half-fill the hole** with planting mix, and gently tread firm. Check that the tree is still at the right depth, then fill the hole up, firm again and level the surface. Attach the tree to its support with an adjustable tie fixed near the top of the stake. Water in well.

Planting a container-grown tree

■ **Mark out the planting position** of the tree, and dig out a hole large enough to allow for 10cm of planting mix below and all round the rootball.
■ **Water the plant thoroughly** and stand it in the hole on the layer of planting mix. Cut down the side of the container and remove it carefully.
■ **Fill in around the rootball** with planting mix, firming it as you go with your fists or a trowel handle; level the surface. Water in.
■ **Position the stake** on the side away from the prevailing wind. Drive it in at a 45° angle to avoid the roots, and secure the tree with an adjustable tie.

Soft fruit

You can plant bush fruits in the same way as tree fruits, following the appropriate bare-rooted or container-grown method described opposite.

Blackcurrants need to be buried 5–8cm lower than their original growing depth to encourage branching from below ground. Staking is usually unnecessary, except for standard redcurrants and gooseberries, which need supporting with stakes and adjustable ties near the top of the stem.

Blackberries, raspberries and fan or cordon-trained gooseberries and currants should be tied in to a system of horizontal wires. These can be attached either to vertical posts, or to vine eyes screwed into a wall or fence.

After planting

Some fruits need pruning at planting time to stimulate plenty of new growth where it is needed. You do not have to prune fruit trees at planting time, unless you are training a fan or espalier from a one-year-old tree. Cut down all stems of blackcurrant to 2–3cm high after planting. Prune the main stems on gooseberry and red or white currant bushes by half, making the cuts just above outward-facing buds. Cut raspberries down to a bud about 23cm above the ground.

The formative years

For best results, keep an area 1m wide weed-free for at least the first two to three seasons. Do this by hoeing, spraying with weedkiller, or by mulching with manure or compost. Water regularly in dry periods, especially if the soil is light; continue until the start of winter for bush fruits, and for one to two years for tree fruits. Feed plants every spring, and prune as appropriate for shapely, productive plants.

Fruit in small spaces

By using compact varieties and restricted forms, you can assemble a large amount of fruit in a small area. A garden about 6 x 4m could include a row each of gooseberries, redcurrants and blackcurrants; two rows of raspberries; loganberries, blackberries, cordon apples and pears, and fan-trained peaches around the perimeter on posts and wires or a 2m fence. In a tiny garden, you could plant cordon apples on very dwarfing rootstocks, 75cm apart against a fence; train three or four raspberry plants in a cluster round a pillar; and plant a thornless cut-leaved blackberry to make an attractive arch. Strawberries are good edging plants, standard gooseberries and redcurrants are decorative highlights in flower borders, and many tree fruits will grow well in generous-sized pots.

82 Apples and pears

IF YOU WERE LUCKY ENOUGH TO GROW UP WITH AN APPLE OR PEAR TREE IN YOUR GARDEN, YOU WILL PROBABLY WANT TO CONTINUE THE TRADITION. THERE IS A SHAPE TO SUIT EVEN THE SMALLEST SPACE, AND TODAY'S DISEASE-RESISTANT VARIETIES MAKE GROWING SUCH FRUIT EASIER THAN EVER BEFORE.

In a larger fruit garden you can grow all kinds of tree types: half standard apple trees such as these are easy to pick from.

Getting the right shape

Trained trees for small gardens Trained flat against a wall or trellis, fruit trees take up relatively little space. Stretching the branches out horizontally produces an espalier tree, while fanning them out from the main branch produces the fan. The 'step-over' – a form of cordon, or single-stemmed tree – is ideal along paths in the vegetable garden.

■ You will need to prune most trees each year or they will lose their structured shape.

Save time on pruning If you don't want to prune every year and only have a small space to grow a fruit tree, plant trees grown on dwarfing rootstocks. Trees on an M27 rootstock will only reach 1.8m and an M9 will reach 2.4m.

■ If you have a large lawn or meadow, buy a half standard or standard tree with a long trunk (1.2–1.5m). You can let them grow relatively freely and prune lightly but regularly in winter every two or three years. This is the only suitable method for quinces, which need only occasional light pruning.

The art of hard pruning This kind of pruning removes quite a lot of wood. It is also known as three-budded pruning since it involves cutting apple and pear trees back to the third bud on fruit-bearing branches, and is recommended for artificially structured apple and pear trees such as cordons, espaliers and fans.

■ You need to take account of how vigorous the tree is before you prune it. If last year's growth was less than 50cm, then it is not a particularly vigorous tree and will benefit from hard pruning. You should prune in winter when the tree is dormant and cut back to three buds on each spur bearer, a lateral branch that grows on a framework or primary branch.

■ If last year's growth was more than 50cm, then you are dealing with a vigorous tree that will be difficult to control with hard pruning. Bend the rules of three-budded pruning and don't cut back as hard, leaving four, five or six buds on each spur bearer.

■ If trees have been neglected, the spur bearers are often multiple and complicated. Don't have any qualms about simplifying them by keeping only those closest to the framework branches.

Natural pruning Today, most commercial fruit growers don't use the hard-pruning method. They usually prefer to manage their trees more naturally, an example you could easily follow.

■ Allow the fruit-bearing branches to produce fruit naturally and then prune a few each year by cutting back to just above a young lateral branch that will replace them. This is known as renewal pruning.

■ If the spur bearers have a lot of fruit buds, you can also prune to limit the amount of fruit produced.

A feast of blossom for plenty of fruit

Where have the flowers gone? The most common reason for a tree failing to flower is overpruning. If you want your trees to flower and produce fruit, put away your secateurs. At the very most, prune lightly, leaving at least six buds on each young branch. Because they are pruned only occasionally, quinces don't tend to suffer from this problem.

■ There is another, natural, reason for a tree not producing blossom – it may be too young. It sometimes takes up to ten years for standard or half standard fruit trees to produce fruit, but only two to three years for smaller standards.

Don't forget about pollination Many apple and pear trees need to be pollinated. In order to produce fruit, the blossom on these trees must be fertilised by other very specific species whose pollen is transferred by bees and other pollinating insects such as butterflies.

Thinning spurs on trained apples and pears

1 Thin fruiting spurs that have become crowded or cross each other by cutting some out at their base, or where they branch.

2 Remove any young shoots and buds that are going to become inaccessible, emerge close to main branches or point in the wrong direction.

3 Aim to leave an open, balanced arrangement of sideshoots to admit plenty of air and light; clear away all prunings when you have finished.

If insects have not done the job of pollination, use a soft, small paintbrush to stroke the centre of each bloom lightly and transfer the pollen from one flower to another.

■ Ensure that the surrounding hedges contain bushes that will attract bees.
■ Attract pollinating butterflies to your garden by providing a saucer of water and a bit of sugar or jam to feed on during the flowering period.

Pollinating companions When planning an orchard, make sure you have varieties that flower at the same time and that one is a good pollinator. 'Conference', 'Doyenne du Comice' and 'Beurré Hardy' are all good pollinating varieties of pear. 'Reine des Reinettes', 'Golden Delicious', 'James Grieve' and 'Cox's Orange Pippin' are pollinating apples. 'Evereste' is a pollinating crab apple. Crab apples have small fruit, only used for making jam or jelly.
■ If there are lots of apple and pear trees growing nearby there is a good chance that they will include varieties that will be able to pollinate your trees.

Getting manure to the roots If you simply spread manure around the base of your trees, most of the nutrients will remain concentrated on the surface of the soil and only a small part will be absorbed quickly. To prevent this from happening, use a crowbar to make a series of holes, 20cm deep, at regular intervals at the base of the crown. Throw one or two handfuls of manure into each hole and water well.

Protecting your fruit

Thin out at the right time If they have been pollinated, all the flowers on an apple or pear tree can set, or form fruit. This will produce lots of tiny apples or pears, so it is essential to remove all but one of the fruitlets in a cluster to achieve good-sized fruits. Keep the fruitlet in the centre of the cluster for apples and one on the edge of the cluster for pears.

Thin out in stages Always thin out in two stages so that you do not traumatise the tree – a surge of sap to the remaining fruits could make them drop.
■ Pears should be thinned out first when the fruitlets are the size of hazelnuts and then again a second time when they have reached the size of walnuts.
■ For apples, the fruit should be thinned out about a month after the tree has flowered, and then a second thinning should follow about a fortnight later.
■ If you only thin out once, it is best to do it at the 'walnut' stage. Do not remove the fruit at the peduncle, or stalk. Instead, cut the pear or apple in half, leaving part of the fruit on the tree.

Wrap a prepared grease band round the trunk to prevent damage by winter moths.

Preventing 'corky' apples There's nothing more unpleasant when you bite into an apple than coming across brown 'corky' patches in the middle of the fruit. These blemishes are caused by a lack of the trace element boron. Using completely natural manure or organic fertiliser will help to prevent these patches, which are often the result of adding large quantities of lime and potassium to the soil.

- If the deficiency is already apparent, try a rescue remedy of seaweed, which is rich in boron. It is available in powder and liquid form, the first for spreading around the base of the tree and the second for spraying on the leaves.

Say goodbye to canker Some varieties of apple tree are susceptible to a disease known as canker, which is particularly virulent in damp conditions and on badly drained soil. The telltale signs to look out for are brownish patches on young branches in winter, followed by the shrinking and cracking of the bark on the larger branches. The edges of the affected areas are transformed into a ridge and, eventually, the branches wither and die.

Great apples and pears

Worcester Pearmain This apple fruits early and freely in September, producing bright red, sweet apples with firm, juicy white flesh. It is frequently used as a pollinator for the favourite 'Cox's Orange Pippin'.

Laxtons Fortune A self-fertile, strongly growing apple, it produces lots of yellow fruits streaked with red that have a flavour similar to a Cox. The trees can be susceptible to canker and may only produce fruit every other year.

Egremont Russet This apple crops heavily from late September to early October, producing golden yellow fruit with broken russet-coloured skin. It has a rich, sweet nutty flavour and crisp texture and keeps for two or three months.

Conference The most widely grown late pear, it crops reliably in October, and keeps well. The fruits have long necks and firm flesh.

Fertility Improved A self-fertile pear, it produces a heavy crop of medium-sized, crisp, juicy and sweet pears in October. The pears can also be used for cooking.

- Cut off and burn any affected young branches and use a pruning knife or well-sharpened knife to cut out the cankers on the larger branches until you expose the healthy wood. Apply a wash made from a mixture of garden soil and water, a product known as pine tar or an anticanker wound sealant.

Weigh down branches to get more apples The formation of fruit buds depends on the circulation of sap, which is in turn dependent on the angle of the branch. A vertical branch is more likely to make new wood than fruit. To reduce the circulation of sap and encourage fruit buds to form, reduce the angle of vertical branches by attaching weights to them such as baskets filled with pebbles or by tying them down with string attached to tent pegs. Try to get them as close to the horizontal as possible.

Pick pears when they part easily from the tree and use only healthy, unblemished fruit for storing. This variety is 'Louise Bonn de Jersey'.

Create an anti-caterpillar belt In May and June, the codling moth lays its eggs on the leaves of young fruit of apple and pear trees. Its larvae – tiny caterpillars that tunnel into the fruit to eat the seeds – will leave your crop incurably worm-eaten.

■ Prevent a second infestation by tying a strip of greased corrugated cardboard around the trunk of each of your apple and pear trees (see page 85). After feasting on your apples, the caterpillars will make their way down the trunk towards the ground where they will nestle in the cardboard, an ideal place for the larvae to turn into moths. In March or April, before the moths emerge from their chrysalises, remove the card and burn it. In this way, you will destroy the next generation of codling moths.

■ Another method of attracting and trapping codling moths is to hang sticky traps in the trees. These are available in various colours which attract different pests, and some have a pheromone scent which makes them even more effective. These sticky traps attract the codling moths, which then get stuck and can be more easily disposed of.

Test apples for ripeness by lifting them gently, rather than by twisting them off.

Support the branches In heavy-cropping years, apple and pear trees can be quite literally weighed down with fruit. When this happens there is a risk of some of the framework branches breaking off.

■ You can prevent this by carefully lifting the branches and propping them on forked supports pushed into the ground.

How to get perfect fruit In the early 20th century, before the introduction of chemical treatments, 'bagging' was widely used by commercial growers to protect their fruit. The method involves encasing each apple and pear – as soon as they reach the size of

Growth buds, spur buds and side shoots

Gardeners who keep a close eye on their fruit trees may notice different types of buds on their trees in winter. These buds indicate how the tree will grow during the coming season, and also determine the best way of pruning it; you would not usually want to remove a flower and fruit bud that will produce the current season's fruit.

Growth bud The simplest type of bud. Small, pointed and slightly swollen, it appears in a leaf axil on the current year's growth. The following year, it produces leaves or new branches.

Spur bud A conical-shaped bud larger than the growth bud from which it comes. It takes another year to become a flower and fruit bud, unless a surge of sap causes it to produce a branch.

Flower and fruit bud The final stage in the development of a growth bud. The relatively large, rounded bud that produces a cluster of flowers will, if all goes well, produce some fruit later in the year.

Side shoot A short, slender branch. Most end in a spur or bud that produces fruit.

Fertile bud A fleshy swelling that forms at the point on the stem where fruit was attached. It is a fertile bud that will produce more fruit.

a walnut – in a paper bag or cone fastened around the stalk with an elastic band. This may be a laborious task but it is worth while and avoids the use of sprays.

■ Fruit protected in this way isn't usually attacked by grubs and caterpillars, doesn't tend to have blemishes, ripens more quickly and is generally larger. You can save up paper bags or make the paper cones from old newspaper.

Storing fruit

Pick at the right time It is the right time to pick your fruit when the first few ripe apples or pears fall, not counting the ones that fall prematurely because they are caterpillar-eaten. Fruit is ripe when it comes away from the branch if twisted slightly.

A useful gadget The fruit picker is a handy piece of equipment. It will save you having to climb or use a ladder when picking fruit at the end of the tallest branches of your trees. Available from garden centres, it consists of a canvas or plastic bag that is fitted onto the end of a 3–4m handle. These bags have pliant prongs around the edge which catch the fruit stems, and with a gentle pull the fruit drops into the bag.

Handle with care Pick apples and pears carefully to avoid bruising them – otherwise they will not keep. Cup the fruit in your hand as you twist it from its branch.

Top tips for long-term storage Always harvest apples and pears in dry weather. It is important to pick all the fruits before the first frosts as they cannot withstand temperatures below –3°C.

■ **Discard damaged fruit** Examine apples carefully and put aside any damaged fruits for stewing.

■ **Pack carefully** Place apples stalk down in a waxed cardboard tray. Make sure they do not touch.

■ **Keep cool and dry** Put the trays in a well-ventilated, sheltered place for a few days so the fruit can really dry out, then store in a cool place such as a garage, cellar or outhouse.

■ **Inspect regularly** Remove any that are beginning to rot.

Composting damaged apples Fallen and damaged fruit usually contains larvae or bacteria, which become active after a few

Apples and pears to eat and keep

Choose carefully and you will be able to eat apples from late summer to the following spring. Varieties that crop early need to be eaten within a week or two of picking; those that crop in October–November keep for longer.

Late summer 'Beauty of Bath', 'Discovery', 'Irish Peach', 'Petit Pippin'.
Early autumn 'Greensleeves' (self-fertile and good pollinator), 'James Grieve' (an excellent cropper that grows well in northern regions), 'Laxton's Fortune', 'Katy'.
Late autumn 'Egremont Russet', 'Lord Lambourne' (self-fertile and reliable heavy cropper), 'Meridian', 'Sunset' (similar to 'Cox's Orange Pippin', but more disease-resistant).
Early winter 'Blenheim Orange' (good as a cooker and eater), 'Crispin', 'Gala', 'Spartan'.
Late winter 'Golden Delicious' (may be biennial), 'Kent', 'Pixie', 'Winston' (self-fertile).
Spring 'Red Pippin' (juicy, Cox-like flavour), 'Granny Smith', 'Josephine', 'May Queen'.

There are three types of pear, based on the season when they are ripe and ready to eat, and their keeping qualities. Summer and autumn pears don't store well. Winter pears are picked in autumn, but will keep until January or February.

Summer pears These ripen in August and September. The best-known are 'Docteur Jules Guyot' and 'Williams Bon Chrétien'.
Autumn pears These are ripe in October and November. This group includes 'Concorde', 'Beurré Hardy', 'Joséphine de Malines' and 'Doyenné du Comice'.
Winter pears These ripen in October and November, but keep through winter if stored well. 'Conference', 'Winter Nelis' and 'Olivier de Serres', are dessert pears; 'Catillac', a culinary pear, keeps until May.

months spent on the surface of the soil and can be a welcome and active addition to the compost heap.

- Collect these apples, stamp on them hard to squash them, and then add them to the heap. The organisms already present in the heap will neutralise any harmful fungi and insects in the fruit, and you will be able to spread your well-rotted compost at the foot of your fruit trees the following autumn.
- Adding fruit to the compost heap also helps to accelerate the rate at which the material breaks down, as the sugar in the apples promotes much faster fermentation of the compost.

Traditional autumn clear up As soon as the leaves begin to fall from your apple and pear trees, run the lawn mower over the grass beneath the trees, leaving the cuttings in place. The shredded leaves will be a real treat for earthworms and will soon disappear into the soil. This is an ideal way of getting rid of all the scab bacteria – a disease that causes unsightly marks on the fruit and leaves – and will help to reduce the following year's contamination.

Clear fallen leaves and fruits and burn or thoroughly compost them to defeat overwintering pests and disease spores.

Storing pears After harvesting pears, place them in fruit crates and leave them to 'sweat' for a few days in a well-ventilated place. Then wrap individually in paper and place carefully on fruit trays, in a cool, airy spot. Pears can be stored at a slightly higher temperature than apples, and keep well in an unused room in the house.

■ For added protection, when the fruits have dried out completely dip the stalks in melted wax and leave them to dry. Removing the fruit stalk opens the way for disease; leave it in place to make the pear keep better and last longer.

Drying apples and pears Remove the core of the fruit and slice into rings about 5mm thick, without removing the peel. Dip each ring into a mixture of water and lemon juice, pat dry and thread onto a cane cut to fit between the shelf rests in your oven. When the cane is full, but not too tightly packed, place it in the oven on a low heat overnight.

It is a good idea to visit specialist fruit nurseries as they will have a far wider choice than general garden centres.

When they are dry, the apple and pear rings can be removed from the cane and stored in paper bags.

Plenty of choice There are more than 2300 varieties of apple, 500 pears, 300 plums and 300 fruit bushes available. To ensure you buy the right variety of fruit for your needs, look out for local fruit-tasting days at nurseries and orchards in your area.

Storing apples

1 Wrap individual fruits loosely in a sheet of newspaper.

2 Place wrapped fruits in a single layer in a shallow wooden or cardboard box. Store in a cool, dry place.

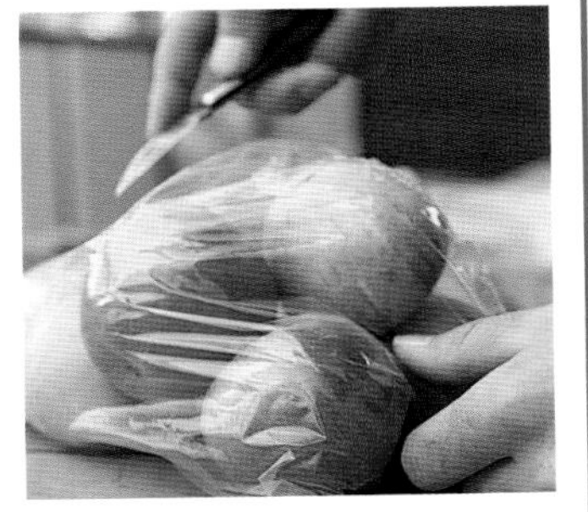

3 Or store apples in plastic bags, pierced to allow in some air; keep no more than three in each bag. Check often for signs of rotting.

90 Growing stone fruit

BY GROWING AN APRICOT, CHERRY, PEACH OR PLUM TREE YOU ARE BRINGING TO YOUR GARDEN SOME OF THE MOST SUCCULENT SUMMER DELICACIES. THESE LUSCIOUS FRUITS WERE COMMONLY GROWN IN THE PAST AND DESERVE ROOM IN THE MODERN GARDEN.

Choosing a stone fruit tree for your garden

The right growing conditions Plum and cherry trees grow well all over the country but require a sunny spot. Both prefer a moisture-retentive, free-draining soil, though cherries are not very successful in dry, sandy ground. Peaches and apricots, however, do require higher temperatures. Both can be grown in East Anglia and the south-east of England trained as a fan against a sunny, protected wall, but rarely do well in the north unless in protected areas of the garden or under glass. In the grand houses of the past, gardeners guaranteed success by growing them in large, unheated, 'lean-to' greenhouses, built against a south-facing wall in a kitchen garden.

The temperamental apricot Even in the most favourable soils, the quantity and quality of an apricot tree's production tends to be unpredictable. It does, however, self-fertilise, so you only need one.

- The apricot tree can blossom as early as February or March, depending on where it is planted, and therefore its flowers are liable to frost damage.
- If a frost is forecast, cover the trees with horticultural fleece.

A potted cherry As gardens get smaller, there is a demand for small cherry trees. The most dwarfing rootstock is Colt, which reduces the height of most varieties to 5m. It isn't common to grow cherries and apricots in pots, but they can be happy in a large container with drainage holes, and rooted in a mixture of slightly clayey garden

Remove suckers from the trunks of cherry and other fruit trees if they appear. Use secateurs and cut them cleanly against the trunk.

Pick cherries as soon as they are ripe, before they are eaten by birds. Prune cherry trees trained on walls in late June and early July.

Apricots for cooler climes

Gold Cott A self-fertile variety with golden-yellow August fruits. It will cope with wet and cold British growing conditions.

Moorpark Large juicy apricots with late July fruits. It is not as hardy as 'Gold Cott' and needs an unheated greenhouse or a sunny, south-facing wall if grown outside. A good choice if you want to grow an old variety: it originated in 1760.

Alfred Medium to large apricots that are orange with a pink flush. Fruit in late July to early August. A vigorous tree.

If possible, plant an apricot tree facing south, south-east or south-west but certainly not east: if you do, blossoms frozen during the night risk being roasted in the morning sun.

soil and a fairly sandy compost. You may have to bring apricots into a greenhouse or conservatory for winter.

The cherry tree – family matters There are three types of cherry tree, which differ considerably in their fruit and overall appearance. Do you want to make jam, or to eat fruit straight from the tree? Make sure you know the difference to avoid planting the wrong type.

- **Sweet cherries** The descendants of the wild cherry tree produce sweet, large fruit which taste delicious straight from the tree. The trees are often far too large for modern or town gardens, but if you have room they are very decorative.
- **Sour or culinary cherries** These acid-tasting fruits with pink, red or white flesh are excellent for jam. They are descendants of the Morello (self-fertile) cherry.
- **'Real' cherries** Hybrids of the two types mentioned above, these cherries are quite large with a moderately acid flavour and tend to ripen late in the season. 'May Duke' is the most well known of this type.

Too tall for picking A cherry tree grafted onto a standard tree, one with a trunk 1.8–2m high, will be more likely to grow tall than the same tree grafted onto a half standard tree with a trunk 1.2–1.5m high. This is something to consider with future harvests in mind, since it is not always easy to pick the cherries growing at the end of high branches.

A smaller cherry tree When grafted onto a wild cherry tree, a cultivated cherry will adapt to most kinds of soil, except excessively chalky ones. However, it will grow as tall as if it had been grafted onto a standard tree, and you could still have trouble reaching some of the branches, even with a ladder.

- To get a smaller tree, no bigger than 7m in height, ask in the nursery for a cherry tree grafted onto a Gisela 5 rootstock. In addition to its reduced size, grafts like this will take well in dry, poor, chalky soils.

Peaches in a pot The blackthorn is a thorny bush very common in the countryside. Years ago gardeners would use it as a rootstock for peach trees. They would shield graft onto it a bud taken from a healthy peach tree, and the result would be a very small tree, which could be cultivated in a large container on a terrace.

A hedge made of plum trees In some regions the plum tree is traditionally used in mixed rural hedges. The variety usually chosen is a wild one called Prunus cerasifera. Small and slightly thorny, it produces a mass of blossoms as winter draws to a close, which result in a multitude of perfectly edible small plums. If you are planting an informal mixed hedge in your garden, adding a few of these could make a tasty difference to the landscape.

Self-fertilising plum trees Some varieties of plum tree can be planted in isolation and produce plums without having to be pollinated by other varieties. These include the large-fruiting 'Jubilee', the cooking plum 'Marjorie's Seedling', the dessert 'Victoria' and the disease-resistant 'Purple Pershore'.

Self-fertile cherries

Celeste A naturally smaller plant with really tasty fruits in early July.Its compact habit is ideal for a smaller garden.

Morello A favourite with the cooks. It fruits in August and, unlike many other fruits, will grow on a north-facing wall. It will pollinate nearly all other cherries.

Stella Tasty dessert fruits ripe for picking in July. This is another variety that will pollinate many other cherries.

Summer Sun The cherry to grow in the North, as it is very hardy. With its tasty fruits that appear in July, this variety is becoming a popular choice for today's gardeners.

Getting the best fruit

How many years must you wait? Once planted, a stone fruit tree will not produce fruit immediately. It needs to develop its framework of branches before its young shoots can become fertile. You will have to wait three to four years before the first fruit appears, but it will take five to ten years, according to the species, before you obtain a substantial yield.

To avoid overloading on a peach tree cut off the early buds that appear at the tips of the last year's shoots.

Juicier apricots Your apricots will be bigger and juicier if you give your tree four to six thorough waterings between May 15 and September 15 during dry weather.

- Water in line with the active roots, in a circle under the outer extent of the foliage.

Rainy day blues If rains continuously as cherries are ripening, there is a risk that they will burst as water is absorbed into the fruit. In rainy areas, choose varieties that are known to be less liable to burst.

- 'Early Rivers', as well as numerous varieties of Morello and other acid cherries are all resilient to this problem.
- To avoid causing bursting yourself, never water cherries just as they are ripening, nor afterwards.

How to ensure an abundance of cherries
Think of the trunk of your cherry tree as a pipe transporting sap to the branches and the fruit. This sap flow is impaired by the bark of the tree, because its circular fibres tighten around the trunk.

■ An old-fashioned tip for improving the flow of sap up the trunk of a young cherry tree is to cut four vertical slits around the trunk about halfway up. This will cause the bark to swell up and rapidly form a new surface, but it will have relieved its stranglehold on the trunk.

A cherry-picking tip The first cherries ripen about 40 days after the tree has blossomed, and for a single variety the harvest lasts for about three weeks. When picking them, avoid tearing off the stalk the cherry hangs on, because that is where the buds will grow that will produce next year's fruit.

Barren plums If your plum tree is not producing fruit, the first thing to consider is whether it is bearing blossom. If a tree does not have any flowers it will not bear fruit.

■ If your plum tree is not producing blossom, it is either because it is still too young – less than three or four years old – or because it is growing too vigorously. If the latter is true, 'calm it down' by sawing off one or two large roots growing just below the surface. To find them, dig a trench part way round the tree beneath the outer edge of the foliage. This is called root pruning.

■ If there are flowers on the tree, the lack of fruit might be caused by the absence of a pollinating variety nearby. If that is the case, you will need to plant a good pollinating plum tree such as 'Oullin's Golden Gage', close by. The absence of fruit might also be the result of bad weather when the tree was in blossom.

Thinning for perfect fruit If the branches of your plum tree are overloaded with fruit, you will need to consider thinning out the overloaded parts to ensure that the remaining fruit develops normally.

■ Do not thin out until after June, which is when the fruit naturally drops. Sometimes things can safely be left to nature.

■ Any fruit that is awkwardly placed or particularly small should be the first to be thinned out. Only keep six to ten fruits per metre on the main branches.

An abundance of blossom is essential to ensure a good crop of fruit later on. Bees (top) will help to pollinate this peach tree. Peach blossom is vulnerable to late frosts and may need protection with horticultural fleece if it appears early. Cherry blossom (below) on wall trained trees may also need shielding from hard frosts.

Planning your plum harvest
When you are choosing plum trees for your

Thin plums to 5-8cm apart in early June and prop up heavily laden branches to prevent breakage. Early plums will need further pruning after they have borne fruit.

garden it is worth bearing in mind when they fruit. If you regularly holiday during August (when most plums ripen) you'll need to plant early or late fruiters, as the fruit won't wait to be picked and you will lose your crop.

An early fruiter is the very old variety 'Mirabelle de Nancy', ripening in early August. The well-known, self-fertile 'Victoria' fruits in late August. Another old favourite, introduced in 1830, is 'Kirke's Blue', which fruits in early September. This old-timer is pollinated by another old variety, the cooking plum 'Czar', which fruits at the same time.

Pruning stone fruit trees

The limits of pruning If your cherry is growing to a giant size, you will not force it to stay small by repeatedly cutting it back. This will limit the cherry crop and harm the tree. You need to replace the tree with one that is naturally smaller.

The right time to prune a cherry If you cut large branches off your cherry tree, you risk exposing it to pests and diseases.

- Help the wounds to heal by pruning from July to the end of September, after the harvest, when the sap is descending. Never prune in winter as silver leaf disease may enter the tree via pruning cuts.
- If you forget to loosen the ties attaching a young cherry tree to its support, the trunk may look quite deformed. Loosen the tie and the trunk will gradually return to its normal shape. If you leave it for years the trunk will be scarred for good.

Autumn clearance After the leaves have fallen, remove all fruit 'mummified' by disease and still on the trees. These shrivelled fruits carry disease and are potential sources of further contamination.

Top tips for pruning peaches When you buy a new peach or nectarine tree, select a well-balanced specimen with at least four healthy laterals. This will make it much easier to perform the essential early pruning, and you will end up with a much better-shaped tree.

- **After planting** In the first spring cut back the main leading shoot just above a strong lateral, leaving at least four healthy laterals. This will avoid a very tall, spindly tree and encourage a neat rounded tree instead.
- **Removing shoots** Take out any shoots that have grown below the main head of the tree, cutting flush with the trunk.
- **Shortening lateral shoots** Cut back by two-thirds to an outward-facing bud. Remove any weak or damaged laterals.
- **Annual pruning** In the second spring, prune the main laterals and sub-laterals by half to an outward-facing bud. Hard annual pruning keeps the tree's growth in check and ensures the tree doesn't become bare in the centre.

Prune your peach trees when they are in blossom With a mature, fruiting tree (usually more than three years old), this is the best way of seeing where to prune, since it is the presence and number of blossoms that determines where to cut. As you cut away sections of branch with blossom on it, you are thinning out the future fruit, so the fruit that remains will be bigger and better. This late pruning also reduces problems from diseases attacking your tree.

Cruel to be kind To ensure that fruit doesn't grow at the ends of the stems on a peach tree, making them spindly and weighing them down, always cut off the early buds that appear at the tips of the previous year's shoots. Spare the fruit-bearing buds at the base of the shoots and you'll get a good crop of peaches and a tidy tree.

The easy-care plum tree The plum does not need to be pruned to produce fruit and does not benefit from having its branches cut back, as this causes it to discharge gum.

- Prune lightly to keep the tree in shape when the sap is falling, between harvest and leaf fall.

Propping an overladen branch In a year when your tree is fruiting heavily, the branches may become bowed down with the fruit. Unless supported, they are liable to break under the weight.

- Rest the branch on a forked piece of wood (right), or strap it to the top of a support, and prop it up against level ground.
- For a branch on a low tree an inverted rake makes a good improvised support.
- Props are not very secure, so watch they don't collapse when the branches are being buffeted by strong winds.

Growing healthy trees

A bitter taste Rue has a reputation for having a bitter taste. Take advantage of this characteristic by planting the perennial at the foot of your stone fruit trees. It will protect them from aphids, which establish their colonies on young shoots. It is thought that a bitter constituent from the rue passes into the tree's sap through its roots, and repels the aphids.

Spotting silver leaf A common problem for plums and cherries: silver leaf is a fungal infection that turns the leaves silver. In advanced cases, the branches may be dead and the bark a home to growths of purple fungi. If the bark of a tree looks healthy but

If a peach tree is heavily laden with fruit, you can support the branches by propping them up with forked stakes, using pads of old sacking to protect the branch, or a rope tied to a central stake.

Early nectarines ripen in July. Check whether the flesh around the stalk is soft, then lift the fruit gently in the palm of your hand. If ready, it will come away easily from the stalk. Later varieties ripen throughout August into early September. They will keep for a few days in a cool place and surplus fruits can be bottled or frozen.

the leaves are silver, the tree may simply be showing signs of needing a general-purpose garden feed.

■ There is no effective treatment for silver leaf, so remove badly blighted branches, preferably in summer, and burn them. Disinfect your pruning knife or secateurs afterwards. If the whole tree is affected it should be felled and burnt. Plums with the 'Pixie' rootstock have a degree of resistance to silver leaf.

A barrier against ants It is usually ants that bring aphids to fruit trees? Ants actually 'import' aphids so that they can consume the sweet honeydew that the aphids secrete when sucking the sap from their host plant. Wrap grease bands, available from garden centres, around the tree trunks to keep the ants and other pests at bay.

■ Check the manufacturer's information for the age of the tree the grease can be used on; young trees may absorb the substance through their developing bark.

Preserve precious calcium Calcium helps fruit stones to form, which is why apricot, cherry, peach and plum trees always benefit from fertiliser rich in the substance, unless the soil is naturally chalky and already rich in calcium carbonate.

■ Make several holes 25–30cm deep around the base of the tree, and pour one or two handfuls of a calcium or lime-rich fertiliser, such as powdered bone, natural phosphate or ground chalk into each hole. Water well. Most modern plant feeds contain calcium.

Beware of broken branches Often, large branches will break off at the base, especially on cherry and plum trees. This is usually because too many large branches were left on the tree when it was young, a problem made worse by the branches rubbing against each other. Prune a tree into shape during the first three years of its life: keep only those branches growing at an angle away from neighbouring ones.

Protect peaches from leaf curl Certain plants have a special protective effect on fruit trees. Plant garlic, nasturtiums or tansy, a yellow-flowered member of the Compositae family, at the foot of your peach trees. This will help to overcome attacks of leaf curl, a very common disease caused by a microscopic fungus.

- Some trace elements help trees to stay healthy. Zinc, for example, is good for peach trees. Gardeners of old would spread a few zinc filings around the foot of their peaches, and rainwater would draw the beneficial metal down to the roots.
- If peach curl is a particular problem in your garden, choose the variety 'Hylands Peach', which has tasty white flesh and was bred to be resistant to peach leaf curl. 'Rochester' has some resistance and will produce a late crop of fruit.

Control whitefly naturally Plant a number of tobacco plants among your fruit trees to attract whitefly. The sticky flowers and foliage are a natural trap.

Protect your apricot trees Apricot trees can be prone to a condition known as verticillium wilt. To help to prevent this problem, do not plant them close to vegetables or dahlias, which often harbour the germs. In case of an attack, which produces a sudden withering of the leaves, it is important to cut off and burn the affected branch or branches as soon as you notice the symptoms.

Fruit trees for all occasions

Peach A fruit tree that was traditionally grown in kitchen gardens. 'Rochester' produces medium-sized fruit at the start of August. 'Peregrine E' ripens in mid-August and has large, highly flavoured fruit.

Cherry Best in a large garden, unless grown on a dwarf rootstock or trained as a fan on a sunny wall. One of the best varieties is 'Stella'.

Plum For a taste of the countryside, the plum has long been a favourite, for example the self-fertile 'Victoria' variety. Gages are also a type of plum. They are generally sweeter but cultivated in the same way. Merton Gage is a lesser known variety; it is self-fertile and ideal for use in desserts.

Nectarine Grown in the same way as a peach tree, 'Lord Napier' is a highly flavoured nectarine with pale green flesh that ripens in early August. Can be grown outdoors.

Are whole branches of your apricot tree failing? This often happens, and it does not mean that your tree is lost. To help it to recover, you need to cut back the old branches quite heavily so that only a few centimetres are left, and preserve any suckers that remain. The stumps will soon start growing again and will produce new stronger branches.

Use a trap for plum-eating larvae To deal specifically with codling moths, whose larvae tunnel into fruit, professional tree growers put pheromone traps in their orchards. A sticky strip, covered with a substance that attracts the males, traps the larvae. These traps are now available to amateur gardeners. The traps kill the moths and so you avoid the need to spray.

98 Growing strawberries

STEEPED IN TRADITION, STRAWBERRIES ARE AN ESSENTIAL FEATURE OF EVERY ENGLISH SUMMER. THE JUICY RED FRUITS CAN BE RAISED IN POTS AND HANGING BASKETS, AS WELL AS THE TRADITIONAL STRAWBERRY PATCH.

Planning for a strawberry patch

How big a patch do you need? It really depends on how many strawberries you want. A single 6m row will keep a family fed through the season, or if you're on your own, plant up a strawberry pot.

Plant early in the season A stem from an axillary bud that grows on the surface and forms roots to produce a new plant is called a stolon. You can replant these from your strawberry patch from July onwards until the end of August.

- If you can propagate from an existing plant, you will have an advantage over those who have to buy young plants, since they are only available in garden centres in September and October. Strawberry plants develop roots and accumulate food reserves between the time of planting and winter, so if they are planted late, or worse still in spring, they will not be productive in their first year.

The right depth Strawberry plants should not be planted deep in the ground. Ensure that the crown – the boundary between the roots and the head of leaves – is just above the soil surface. Dig a fairly wide hole, and spread out the roots before covering them with soil and packing it down. No matter how many you have to plant, don't be

Perpetual strawberries often continue fruiting until the first frosts or later if you protect the plants with cloches or fleece. Do not cut plants down after fruiting but simply tidy them by removing all mulching material and weeds and lightly fork over the soil between plants.

Pot-grown strawberries need regular watering. In a dry autumn you should also water summer-planted strawberries frequently.

Root runners for replacement plants by pegging down the small plantlets in the soil or in plunged pots of compost.

tempted to use a dibber as the holes it creates will be too narrow.

Planting a new strawberry bed

1 Rake in general fertiliser just before planting, then mark out planting positions every 38-45cm in rows 75cm apart, using string and canes. Plant at the same level as the pot compost.

2 Firm plants in well and water regularly in dry weather during the first few weeks. Try to complete planting by mid-September.

Rediscover the old flavours Specialist suppliers still have old-fashioned strawberry varieties that were created above all else to please the palate. Their tender fruit is best savoured fresh from the garden.

- Old varieties of strawberry include 'Royal Sovereign' (early), 'Redgauntlet' (midseason) and 'Talisman' (late).

Modern varieties More recent varieties have been bred to grow vigorously, resist disease and improve fruit appearance, but often at the expense of the flavour. New varieties that are readily available include 'Calypso', 'Gorella' and 'Elvira'.

Delicate seedlings When up-rooted from the ground, young strawberry plants are quick to dry out. Do not leave them lying around in the sun. Instead, put their roots straight into a mixture of potting compost and water, and plant them again as soon as possible.

Plant your strawberries on a ridge If the soil in your garden is heavy and wet, it is not the ideal situation for growing strawberries. So when you prepare your strawberry patch, make sure you provide well-drained soil for the roots. For a double line of plants, build up a flat-topped ridge of soil about 20cm high and 1m wide, and set the plants in that.

Strawberries on the patio All is not lost if you love strawberries but have only a balcony or a patio. You can grow them in special strawberry pots with honeycomb cavities, in a graduated stack of terracotta pots, or in large tubs or barrels filled with a mixture of well-decomposed compost and sand, or rich but light earth. Place them in a fairly shady spot, make sure that they never lack water, and regularly remove the stolons so that the plants do not become exhausted. Enjoy the crop – but don't expect to have enough to make jam.

The truth about double-cropping strawberry plants Don't be deceived by the term 'double-cropping', which is used to describe some varieties of strawberry plant.

It is, in fact, rare for strawberries to produce two harvests worthy of the name. Sacrifice the first flowers in order to improve the second crop, and consider the double-cropping strawberry plant simply as a single-cropping one that bears fruit later than the actual single-cropping varieties.

Greenhouse-raised strawberries often flower before many pollinating insects are about. On warm days, you can encourage them in; otherwise you will need to fertilise the open flowers yourself.

Strawberries at home in the woods Originally the strawberry grew in forest clearings, which is why it particularly likes the rather acidic qualities of tree humus.

- Fertilise your strawberry patch by spreading a generous layer of leaf mould over it.
- A reliable traditional tip is to cover the soil between the stalks of the plants with conifer needles, ferns and ground pine bark or, failing that, a good layer of straw. This porous carpet has the added advantage of discouraging weeds and purifying the surface of the soil so that your strawberry plants will be less vulnerable to grey mould and slugs.

Take off the leaves The leaf diseases that strike strawberry plants occur in late autumn. So, as soon as possible after the harvest, clip off their leaves, taking care to cut high enough not to touch the heart of the plants. Your plants will soon grow healthy new leaves.

Dividing alpine strawberries

1 Shear off the old foliage during early March and dig up the clump with a fork.

2 Either cut a plant into several portions or simply tear it apart with your hands; discard the old woody centre.

3 Replant the young outer portions about 30cm apart in fresh ground that has been dug and manured. They make an attractive edging to a bed.

Susceptibility to weeds One of the main problems with growing strawberry plants is their vulnerability to vigorous weeds such as convolvulus, couch grass and buttercups.

The plants are quickly suffocated by the weeds, their fruit is deprived of sunlight and their soil loses its richness. If weeds start to become a serious problem in your strawberry patch you may have to move it to a new, weed-free site.

Combination planting Use the soft, loose soil between two rows of strawberry plants for a line of spinach, white onions or lettuces: crops that are not greedy and will not rob the strawberry plants of nutrients.

Keep their hats on Never hull strawberries before washing them. If you do, the berries will soak up water, which spoils their delicious flavour.

These early strawberries need to ripen considerably before they are ready to pick. Ripe fruit is firm but gently yielding.

The tastiest strawberries

All of the varieties listed below have been specially developed for their excellent flavour.

Cambridge Favourite An early strawberry that produces large, firm fruit for a long period in midsummer; it is a vigorous and reliable plant.

Elsanta An early cropper whose fruits are often sold commercially, but taste better when eaten straight from the plant. The fruits are ready for picking from late spring to midsummer.

Aromel A double-cropper which produces fruits in June–July and August–September.

Symphony A late variety, that is perfect if you like to have strawberries to eat beyond the Wimbledon fortnight. It is not a fussy plant, so is a great option for less than ideal growing conditions. It has an outstanding flavour.

102 Berries from the bush

FILLING A BASKET WITH RASPBERRIES, BLUEBERRIES, CURRANTS, GOOSEBERRIES AND BLACKBERRIES IS A JOYFUL REMINDER OF SIMPLER TIMES. YOU DON'T NEED A LARGE GARDEN TO ENJOY THESE FRUITS, AND ONCE YOU'VE GROWN A FEW YOU WILL BE HOOKED.

Raspberries and blueberries

Mulch the soil for a good crop The raspberry is a woodland plant that benefits from a mulch of partially composted dead leaves, twigs, straw, tree bark, wood shavings, pine needles or any other woody debris. Added on a regular basis, these materials will decompose and create the acidity that the plant needs to grow. Mulching also provides protection against diseases such as spur blight and helps to keep weed growth down.

Raspberries need support Raspberry stems, or canes, are extremely supple and liable to be flattened by wind, rain and the weight of the fruit. It is essential to provide some kind of support such as a post-and-wire system.

- Sink two posts into the ground at either end of the row of canes, reinforcing each one with an angled strut.
- Stretch a length of galvanised wire between the posts, at a height of about 1.7m. Then tighten one end using a straining bolt.
- Tie each cane to the wire with a plastic tie or a piece of garden twine.

Raspberries are ripe when the red fruits feel yielding but not too firm or too squashy. Harvest them regularly as they ripen.

Pruning raspberries Regular pruning ensures a succession of healthy new canes

Easy-to-grow raspberries

SUMMER-FRUITING VARIETIES – EARLY JULY

Glen Clova An old favourite with high yields of fruit; the fruits are small, so ideal for freezing.

Glen Moy A popular choice as it is spine-free, has large berries and produces plenty of fruit.

SUMMER-FRUITING VARIETIES –LATE JULY

Leo Tangy but tasty orange-red fruits; aphid resistant.

Malling Admiral A good all-rounder; doesn't do well in wet soil but is resistant to spur blight.

AUTUMN-FRUITING VARIETIES

Autumn Bliss A self-supporting variety with good flavour; fruits ripen from August onwards.

Fallgold A late variety with yellow fruit.

Heritage A high-yield variety with an average flavour; second harvest from late August until the first frosts.

September An aromatic fruit with a slightly sharp taste; second harvest in September–October.

Zeva A well-known, large-fruited variety; second harvest in September–October.

and good fruit production. When and how you prune depends on the type of raspberry.

- **Summer-fruiting varieties** Once fruiting is over, cut the canes that have just fruited down to ground level. Tie in canes that have grown during the current season. The following spring, cut back the tips on the new canes to a healthy bud.
- **Autumn-fruiting varieties** Prune in February, cutting all the canes down to ground level.

Combating raspberry beetle This pest is often spotted when you are picking the ripe fruit. Keep an eye out for the adult beetles, which lay their eggs on the flowers, and for the brown grubs, which burrow into the centre of the fruit.

- A traditional way to prevent the problem is to plant forget-me-nots (*Myosotis*) next to your raspberries. They self-seed readily and will act as a deterrent.
- Inspect your raspberries regularly during summer. Make your way along the row, tapping the foliage and collecting any beetles in a bowl held beneath the leaves. Then all you have to do is take away the insects and destroy them.

Blueberry history The American blueberry (*Vaccinum corymbosum*) is a modern variety, far more productive than the European species (*Vaccinum myrtillus*), although some say it has less flavour. The European blueberry, or bilberry, grows wild in many European countries, including Britain. It is extremely difficult to grow outside its natural habitat, so in a garden the American blueberry may be a better choice.

- The American blueberry reaches 1–2m high and produces 1–3kg (and sometimes as much as 10kg) of fruit per bush. It is very decorative in autumn.
- Unlike the European blueberry, which grows happily in woodland, the American variety only fruits well in full sun, so choose its position carefully.

Blueberries need acid soil Like its wild counterpart, which grows on peaty heaths, the cultivated blueberry needs an acid soil.

- You will be able to identify your soil type by looking at the local flora. Bracken, gorse, broom and foxgloves are all acid-lovers.
- If you don't have the right soil, you can grow blueberries in a large container of ericaceous compost.

Planting raspberry canes

1 Plant raspberry canes in autumn. Add well-rotted manure to the base of the planting hole and, if the soil is dry or chalky, mix in a quantity of ericaceous compost.

2 Plant only about 10cm deep and spread the roots out. Planting too deep inhibits the development of beneficial suckers. Firm the soil around the base of the canes.

3 Leave a hollow around the base of each plant, and water well. Once the plant has settled in, cut down the canes to 25cm high, cutting at an angle above a bud.

Pick blueberries carefully by hand using a large shallow basket or container so that they do not get crushed or bruised.

■ When planting blueberry bushes, dig a hole 50cm across and fill it with a mixture of equal parts ericaceous compost, leaf or pine-needle mould and well-rotted garden compost. Leave 1.5m between plants.
■ Give the plants an annual top-dressing of moss peat or acid leaf mould to enrich the soil. Alternatively, feed them with an ericaceous plant food.

Always pick blueberries by hand Don't be tempted to use any of the contraptions which are available for gathering wild fruit. Apart from the fact that they gather as many leaves as berries, they will damage berries of the large-fruited cultivated varieties. There is only one solution – lots of patience and picking by hand.

Blueberry pairing Cultivated blueberries require a pollinating partner to ensure a good crop of fruits. Therefore, you need to plant two different varieties, making sure they will flower at the same time to ensure cross-pollination. Choose between early varieties, such as 'Bluetta', 'Duke', 'Patriot' and 'Bluecrop', whose fruit ripens in July, and later varieties, such as 'Nelson' and 'Brigitta', which ripen in August and September.

Autumn and summer-fruiting raspberries The perennial raspberry sends up new shoots from its underground roots at different times of the year, depending on whether it is summer or autumn fruiting.
■ **Summer-fruiting varieties** These fruit once a year, in summer. As some of the shoots bear fruit, others are growing and developing. The new shoots will bear fruit the following year, while the current fruit-bearing shoots will die off.
■ **Autumn-fruiting varieties** The fruit appears from September until the first frosts, on canes that have developed in the current year.

Currants and gooseberries

Planted to perfection Plant young redcurrant or blackcurrant bushes deeply. If the neck of the plant – where the roots join the branches – is 5–10cm below the surface of the soil, it will produce a number of suckers which will later become the important framework branches.
■ Twelve is the ideal number of branches for a blackcurrant or redcurrant bush to encourage maximum fruiting.

Plant cuttings in situ If a friend has a currant bush you admire, ask for a cutting. In early spring, clear and break down the soil in the spot chosen for the new bush and push two 25–30cm long cuttings, taken from the previous year's growth, into the ground. The cuttings should be pushed in at an angle, 10cm apart, with one bud showing.
■ Planting cuttings directly in their growing positions will encourage the plants to put out

deep roots. This will make the young bushes less susceptible to drought than if they are transplanted as baby bushes.

Turning a cutting into a fruiting bush When growing a new bush from a cutting, cut it back every winter for three years before allowing it to fruit.

- **The first winter** After planting, cut back new shoots that have developed to two buds.
- **The second winter** Cut back any new shoots to three buds, and any suckers to 15cm above ground level.
- **The third winter** Cut back shoots to four buds above their base and suckers to 15cm above ground level. The following year, your currant bush will be ready to produce fruit.

Ensuring healthy redcurrants The caterpillars of the currant clearwing moth tunnel into the pith of the shoots of currant bushes. In autumn, cut out and burn any dry, brittle twigs to destroy the larvae.

Watch out, birds about It won't take long for the local bird population to spot your new fruit bushes. They can quickly rob the plant of its fruit or strip the buds from the branches, leaving bare unproductive wood.

- There are deterrents such as vibrating tape, which is effective, but only for a few days. It has to be changed regularly or the birds simply get used to it.
- If you are growing a number of fruit bushes, it is worth building a fruit frame and covering it with fine netting to keep the birds away.

Outwitting the birds Blackbirds and starlings love soft, red fruit. You can outwit them by choosing white and pink varieties of currant such as 'White Versailles' and 'White Dutch'.

Aromatic blackcurrants The blackcurrant is the king of aromatic fruits. It is at its best and produces the sweetest aroma in rich

Blackcurrants are easy to grow and provide one of the richest sources of vitamin C of any fruit.

Red and white currants ripen from early July. Pick whole strings of fruit and remove individual currants with a table fork.

Great-tasting currants and berries

Jonkheer van Tets One of the first redcurrants to ripen in early July, producing large crops of succulent fruit.

Bluecrop A heavy-cropping blueberry that has large, pale blue berries. It is fast-growing and vigorous.

Black Satin For dessert fruits, grow this thornless blackberry with large, black shiny berries that are quite acidic.

Zeva Generous crops of large raspberries grow on self-supporting canes. Fruits ripen in September–October.

Invicta An easy-to-grow gooseberry with almost hairless, pale green fruits. It has some resistance to gooseberry mildew.

Ben Lomond A late-fruiting blackcurrant. The original of the 'Ben' varieties, it is the parent of other 'Ben' blackcurrants.

alkaline soil, but if your soil isn't limy, add some crushed limestone to the soil used to fill the planting hole.

■ France is famed for cassis, a heady blackcurrant liqueur. A traditional tip for stimulating the aroma of blackcurrants is to spread pieces of old plaster around the base of the bushes in winter. As the plaster is broken down by the winter frosts, the calcium sulphate from which it is made will easily be absorbed by the roots.

An ornamental currant Currants aren't grown just for their fruits: many have valuable decorative qualities. *Ribes odoratum* has wonderful yellow flowers in spring, followed by inedible purple fruits and a later show of autumn colour. *Ribes sanguineum* is often planted as part of an informal mixed hedge for its red-pink, late spring flowers.

Failure to fruit Modern varieties of blackcurrant are fairly reliable. However, if there is a year when fruit is sparse, it may be because pollen has been washed off plants by rain, winds or frost. Don't give up, hope for dry weather next year.

New varieties of blackcurrant Many of the very old varieties of blackcurrant have been overtaken by new introductions. Most older varieties flowered and produced fruitlets as early as April. As a result, they were often damaged by frost and their yield was variable. To solve this problem, plant breeders introduced the 'Ben' group, which flowers much later and is less prone to frost damage. These newer varieties, such as 'Ben More', have made growing blackcurrants far easier. This variety has large black shiny fruits with a sweet acid flavour, high in vitamin C, and has resistance to mildew and leaf-curling midge.

Plan for fruits all summer Traditionally, redcurrants ripen from mid June to the end of July, depending on the variety.

■ To have fruit all summer long plant a selection of different varieties. The following are in order of ripening, from the earliest to the latest: 'Jonkheer van Tets', 'Junifer', 'Laxton's Number One', 'Red Lake', 'White Versailles' and 'Rondom'. However, there are also August-fruiting varieties such as 'Redstart' and 'Rovada', which will extend your crop further.

A standard currant If you want a currant that can be picked standing up, takes up little space and is easy to weed around the base, turn the cutting into a standard bush.

■ Remove all the buds from the lower half of the cutting, so that shoots do not develop

Pick fully ripened gooseberries carefully, as they are soft and burst easily. They ripen unevenly so check bushes several times a week.

below ground. Push the cutting vertically into the ground at the chosen position.

- Once it has rooted and new shoots have developed, tie the strongest shoot to a bamboo cane and remove the rest.
- Allow the stem to grow to about 1m, then prune the tip. Side shoots will grow from the top three or four buds.

Rejuvenating currant bushes The simplest way to give new vigour to an old currant bush is to cut all the branches back to ground level in winter. The following spring, a number of suckers or shoots will emerge from the soil and develop during summer. The bushes should begin to bear fruit the following year.

Growing gooseberries Synonymous with an old-fashioned British summer, gooseberries are fortunately very easy to grow in any type of well-drained but moisture-retaining soil. Although gooseberries thrive in full sun or partial shade, they should not be planted in areas which act as frost pockets – they flower in early March and may be damaged by a severe late frost.

Pruning gooseberries the simple way You will need to wear leather gloves when pruning all but the thornless gooseberries. You should prune during autumn or winter, but if birds are likely to damage buds, delay pruning until bud-burst so they do not strip the few remaining buds.

- Cut out dead wood and any crossing branches, and cut back by half any new growth shooting from the main branches.
- In late June cut back newly produced side shoots to four or five leaves from the base.
- Aim to create a plant with a good goblet shape, to make picking easier, and with space in the centre of the bush so that air can circulate around the fruit, helping to prevent disease.

Gooseberries without thorns To make picking less painful, it is worth looking for thornless varieties of gooseberries such as 'Captivator'. This variety is also resistant to powdery mildew, a disease that often affects gooseberries.

Growing for cooking or for eating? There are two types of gooseberry – culinary and dessert. Culinary varieties are ideal for cooking but have too sharp a taste to eat straight from the bush. Dessert gooseberries are sweeter and can be eaten fresh. If you don't have much room, choose a dessert type as younger fruits can be used for cooking and ripe fruits for eating fresh.

Strange fruit The blackcurrant and the gooseberry, have been hybridised to produced the Worcesterberry, *Ribes divaricatum*, a small black 'gooseberry' that tastes of blackcurrant.

Blackberries

Pain-free brambles The thornless blackberry is a cultivar of the familiar wild blackberry. It is the product of genetics and pure chance, since the 'thornless' gene does in fact exist in several species of wild American blackberries. By hybridising various combinations of these species, breeders produced thornless varieties. The fruit of the cultivar doesn't taste as sweet as that of the wild bramble, but it is larger and easier to pick, and there are now several varieties to choose from.

As nature intended In the past, gardeners would have avoided growing the rampant blackberry and simply collected fruits from the hedgerows. Now that there are more compact hybrids available they deserve a place in our gardens.

■ When planting a mixed hedge in a cottage garden, or even a vegetable garden, add a few blackberries and enjoy picking them the traditional way – from the hedgerow.

They are not fussy Blackberries can be grown in most conditions. If you have had trouble growing berried fruit in the past then this is one to try, especially as they are hardy and will even put up with a bit of shade, making them ideal for gardeners who are surrounded by overhanging trees. They would thrive in a woodland setting alongside bluebells and cranesbill, where the free-draining, moist acid soil suits them.

■ As blackberries do not flower until June, they can even be planted in a frost hollow.

One for the birds Normally, gardeners would jealously guard their fruit bushes from the marauding birds that love them so much. Blackberries are such prolific producers that you can afford to share them – you don't need bird-scarers or fruit cages.

■ Because blackberries are so rampant, you will need to cut them back from time to time. But make sure you don't disturb any nesting birds in the process.

A natural rooting hormone Like their wild counterparts, blackberry cultivars produce roots at the point where their stems touch the ground, from which new plants will grow. This is known as propagation by natural layering, and the new roots contain a hormone that makes them very vigorous.

■ Use this organic boost when you are propagating any new plants from cuttings. Cut off some of the small white roots, chop finely and leave to macerate in the water in which you are soaking your cuttings. After 24 hours, you can plant your cuttings with every chance of success, thanks to the hormones in the young blackberry roots.

The growing cycle – the key to pruning During the first year of a blackberry's development, the root stock produces shoots that emerge from the soil and put on several metres growth. The next year, lateral shoots appear on the long climbing stems. These shoots flower and produce fruit during the

Cultivated blackberries have larger fruit than wild plants and a range of varieties now offers fruit from late summer until the frosts.

Blackberries without thorns

Blackberries are extremely tolerant of site and soil conditions, although thornless varieties are fussier than their prickly cousins. Give them the best possible start by planting in moist, well-drained soil in a sunny spot.

Black Satin Vigorous, productive and hardy with large, black, conical fruits of exceptional quality. Harvest from early August for 4–6 weeks.

Merton Thornless An ideal variety for a small garden as it has short canes. The fruits are of a good flavour but it's not a heavy cropper. Fruit will be ripe for picking in August and September.

Oregon Thornless A very popular variety, decorative enough to grow over a trellis, thanks to its coloured autumn leaves. The small to medium-sized fruits have a mild, sweet flavour and are ready to harvest from late August to the end of September.

summer and then die off in winter. During this time, other vigorous shoots will develop from the root stock and produce fruit the following year.

■ When you are pruning, cut out dry, dead stems at the base. Leave all visible new shoots as they wll produce the following summer's fruit.

How to prune blackberries

1 Prune in early spring. Start by cutting out two-year-old stems at the base. Then remove spindly growth from the end of new canes.

2 If you have few new canes, leave some old canes in place to fruit again. Cut back any damage on these old canes to a healthy bud.

3 Remove damaged and diseased wood and any canes that you feel will obstruct paths.

4 Carefully tie in the new year-old stems as these are the ones that will produce the most fruit. They will be cut off at the base the following year.

Support required Even a modern compact variety of blackberry can put on several metres growth in a single season. It is essential to provide its supple climbing stems with support so that they don't sprawl all over the ground. You can, however, wait for a year after planting before putting a support system in place.

■ Sink wood or metal stakes at least 2m long into the ground at 5m intervals and, if possible, support each one with an angled strut. Then stretch three lengths of thick, galvanised wire horizontally between the stakes at a height of 1m, 1.3m and 1.6m above the ground. Tighten each wire at one end with a straining bolt. Finally, plant blackberries along the support system at intervals of 2.5m.

■ As the shoots grow, tie them to the wires at an angle using soft, pliable ties that won't damage the young stems. You can buy practical, reusable ties from garden centres. Alternatively you can use strips of fabric or old nylon tights.

In cold regions Here's a technique that has been used for many years and still works well today. In regions where winter frosts could prove fatal for young blackberry shoots, bend the stems, lay them flat along the row in autumn and protect with a layer of straw, dead leaves or bracken.

Keep out of the sun Once blackberries are picked, they tend to turn red and hard if left in the sun. Cover your crop with a tea towel while you are picking, and keep them in the refrigerator until you use them.

A rose by any other name Blackberry blossom is large and lasts for several weeks – many cottage gardens had a trellis covered in blackberries for the beauty of the blossom as well as for the bounty of the fruit.

110 Growing grapes

VINES HAVE BEEN CULTIVATED IN BRITAIN FOR CENTURIES. IN GREENHOUSES OR SHELTERED GARDENS, A NUMBER OF VARIETIES OF GRAPES ARE EASY TO GROW, AND PRODUCE EXCELLENT CROPS OF FRUIT.

Sweet, succulent grapes

Grow a vine in a pot Fill a large pot 35–40cm in diameter with a mixture of 50 per cent garden soil, 25 per cent soil-based compost and 25 per cent coarse sand. Plant a young vine whose climbing stems can be trained up a pergola or trellis. It will do well on your patio in a sunny position. At the end of summer you will be able to pick a few bunches of delicious table grapes.

■ Repot the vine every two years if possible or replace the first few centimetres of soil with fresh compost mixture.

In the past many large estates had glasshouses dedicated to grape vines. By paying great attention to the temperature requirements of each vine they could produce grapes nearly all year round.

Do you live in a vine-growing region? Like all cultivated plants, the vine has climatic requirements, especially when it comes to summer temperatures. While it can withstand extremely cold winters, it does not like late spring frosts, which destroy the buds, and it needs warmth and baking sun during the summer months to ripen the fruits. Vines planted in the south have a greater chance of success than those grown in the north. Plant against a south-facing wall where they will have shelter and sun.

Get a good grape harvest

To get plump, perfectly shaped dessert grapes, thin the bunches when the fruit first appears by removing damaged or diseased grapes. You don't have to thin grapes being grown for wine.

■ **Let the sun in** As the fruit ripens, tie back, or remove some of the foliage.

■ **Pick on time** When the stem that attaches the bunch to the vine starts to go brown, the fruit is ready for picking.

■ **Cut a branch** Take the whole bunch: they are easier to store and should last longer.

■ **Store well** Put in a box with a soft lining and store in a cool, shaded place for up to a month.

Vines for wine Grapes have been grown for hundreds and hundreds of years in Britain. They do need plenty of attention, so often become a specialist hobby for gardeners, especially those who fancy making their own wine. A well-loved vine will produce grapes for decades but can take up to four years to give you a substantial crop.

■ **The best time to plant vines** Plant vines in November and December. Whether the plant has a rootball or is bare-rooted, make sure the point where it has been grafted onto the rootstock is about 4cm above the level of the soil.

■ If you experience very cold winters, or live in a frost pocket, protect the upper part of the plant by earthing up sand or light soil to cover the graft – or the lower buds where there is no graft. Remove in spring, after the risk of frost has passed.

The best time to prune A trellised vine should be pruned when it starts to produce leaves in March. In cooler northern regions this will prevent damage by late April frosts. It will also preserve the buds at the base, which will go on to develop later.

Rejuvenating an old vine Once a vine reaches 20–25 years old it becomes less productive. Hard pruning will promote new vigour, but should be carried out over two years so that it is less traumatic for the vine.
■ During the first summer, deal with the vine's leaf and grape-bearing shoots that originate near the base of the vine – these are the ones you will keep. Train them in the best direction by staking and trellising.
■ In winter, cut out some of the vine shoots, leaving those produced by the branches you have decided to keep.
■ The following winter, use a saw to cut the vine stock, or trunk, just above the shoots to be retained. Smooth off the cut with a well-sharpened knife or pruning knife and seal with candle wax to prevent infection from pests and diseases.

Protect grapes This is an old-fashioned tip that can help to improve the quality and quantity of your crop. Before your grapes ripen, protect them from wasps and birds by wrapping them in paper bags pierced with holes.

Get grapes until Christmas Cut individual bunches from the vine with a 30cm section of stem on either side. Place one end of the stem in water in a large wine bottle and seal the other end using candle wax. Drop a piece of charcoal in the water to purify it. Store in a cool, dry, well-ventilated room.

Indoor vines If you are intending to grow grapes in a greenhouse, it must face south or south-west. If your greenhouse is unheated, choose varieties that do not require extra heating, such as 'Chasselas d'Or', and maintain frost-free conditions. Allow space above head height for training and plenty of ventilation.

Pruning a vine in March

1 Cutting cleanly at an angle, remove all the branches that bore fruit the previous year.

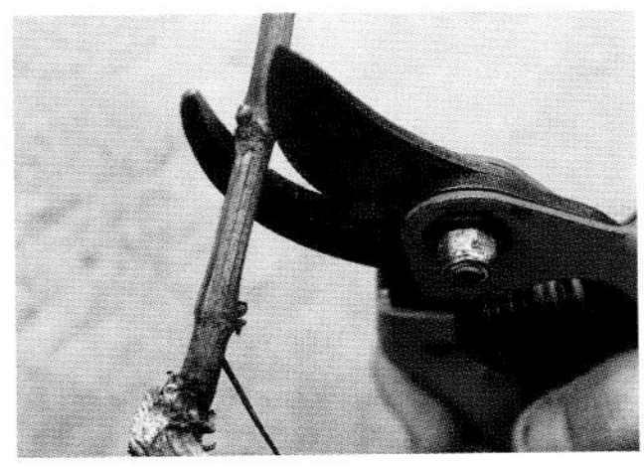

2 Cut back the spurs you are keeping to the second bud. The top bud will produce the fruit.

3 Cut back a long lateral shoot to 20cm and tie it carefully to the training wires. This will extend the vine.

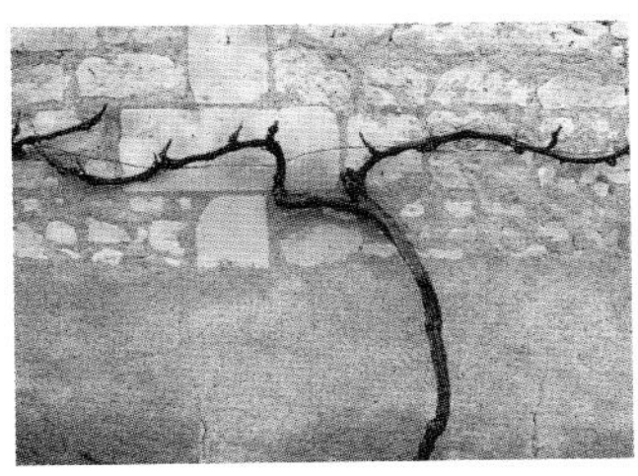

4 De-bud the vine later in the year by removing surplus shoots in summer.

112 Old-fashioned fruits

FIG AND CITRUS TREES WERE 19TH-CENTURY FAVOURITES THAT ARE NOW ENJOYING SOMETHING OF A REVIVAL. TO BE SUCCESSFUL WITH THESE FRUITS YOU MUST TAKE A LITTLE EXTRA CARE, BUT THERE ARE SOME TRIED-AND-TESTED TECHNIQUES TO HELP YOU TO ESTABLISH THEM IN YOUR GARDEN OR CONSERVATORY.

Fig trees have large leaves and may cast too much shade over other greenhouse plants. But if you have space they will produce abundant fruit under glass.

Growing a fig tree

A successful crop The good news about growing figs is that they do not require a pollinating partner and they can grow in nearly all British soils, as long as they are free-draining. Also, pests and diseases rarely affect them. Growing figs only gets complicated when you want to harvest fruit every year rather than growing them simply as an ornamental plant.

- To produce a good crop of fruit the roots need to be restricted by either growing the tree in a pot or by lining the planting hole with paving slabs.
- In the south of England figs will grow happily against a sunny wall, while in the Midlands you can have success if you find a really sheltered, sunny spot. Figs will need protection from the frost to avoid damage – nowadays this can easily be done by covering with horticultural fleece.

The most commonly sold fig for outdoor use is the very hardy 'Brown Turkey', a variety that ripens in August to September. Another hardy fig is 'White Marseilles', which has early fruit with white flesh and an excellent flavour. This fig is often successfully grown in a pot. In the greenhouse opt for 'Rouge de Bordeaux', which has purplish-green fruits. Figs are commonly sold already fan-trained for planting against a wall.

Although particular about climate, the fig tree, once settled, grows happily in the most barren of city garden soils.

- The best time to plant is in early spring when the risk of heavy frosts has passed. Plant in a deep hole with a layer of stones at the bottom and paving slabs to the sides to restrict root growth. Water copiously in its first summer.

Low-maintenance pruning Mature figs need little pruning – just remove any shoots that are crowding each other and preventing a good airflow around the branches.

- After the first crop on a new tree, pinch out the lateral shoots, leaving a shoot with four leaves on. This will encourage replacement fruit-producing stems.

Growing figs in a barrel If you intend to move house in the near future plant your fig in a barrel so it can go with you. The barrel should have a capacity of at least 50 litres and be filled with ordinary soil. It also needs to have handles so you can move it about, and drainage holes drilled in the bottom.

■ Place the barrel with its plant in a cool, well-aired, frost-free place as soon as the leaves start to fall, and keep it there until the following May before moving it to a sheltered spot.
■ Ensure that the soil does not dry out.

Winter protection As long as it is not too big, you can protect the branches of your fig tree from heavy frosts. Draw the branches together, tie them with rope and cover for winter with corrugated cardboard, plastic bubble wrap or garden fleece. Pile up leaves as a warming mulch around the base.

Taking cuttings from a fig tree In winter cut off one of the previous year's shoots complete with its heel – a fragment of bark – and a terminal bud. Plant it out protecting it from frost with dead leaves or straw.

Orange and lemon trees

Citrus trees need winter warmth These trees are the least hardy species grown in Britain and cannot tolerate temperatures below zero. Don't plant them outdoors.

Planting in pots Citrus trees were once the speciality of gardeners who worked in stately homes and had access to an orangery, where these delicate plants could spend winter. However, a conservatory can be just as effective.
■ Plant citrus trees in large pots or tubs with 50cm sides and fill with appropriate compost. Bring them indoors in September and keep them there until the end of May so that they escape the frosts.
■ Water citrus trees twice a week with soft water (rainwater is ideal) until the warm, dry weather returns.

The right fertiliser for citrus trees A balanced mixture of clayey soil, river soil, fine sharp sand, coarse sand and very well-rotted manure does the job admirably. It is not always easy to find all these different ingredients, Special citrus fertilisers are available commercially as well as soluble fertilisers for use when watering.

Treatment for falling leaves If the leaves of your container-grown orange or lemon tree shrivel up and fall, it could be the result of too much water, lack of light, a sudden change in temperature or a very dry atmosphere. Place the pot on a bed of wet gravel, only water when the compost has dried out, and spray the leaves as often as possible with lukewarm water. The fallen leaves will soon be replaced by new ones.

Get a sterile orange tree to bear fruit An old-fashioned treatment was to give it zinc, a trace element sometimes lacking in soil.
■ To enable the beneficial metal to pass into the tree's sap, cut a slit in the bark with a very sharp knife and insert a pinch of zinc filings. Your orange tree will be encouraged to develop flowers and will eventually fruit.

Away from their favoured Mediterranean climate, there are varieties of orange and lemon trees that can be grown on a large pot on a verandah or in a conservatory.

Pests and diseases

THERE IS NOTHING MORE SATISFYING THAN GROWING AND EATING YOUR OWN FRUIT. BUT THIS SATISFACTION IS CAN BE CUT SHORT IF THERE IS A BUG INSIDE. THE FOLLOWING ARE SOME OF THE COMMONEST INSECTS AND DISEASES THAT AFFECT FRUIT TREES AND BUSHES ALONG WITH THE MOST EFFECTIVE, PRIMARILY ORGANIC, WAYS OF DEALING WITH THEM.

Roots

CROWN GALL

This bacterial disease causes whitish swellings on the roots of trees and at the base of the trunk. The swellings can grow as large as footballs, then turn black and rot. The vigour of the tree is not affected and there are no signs of disease on the leaves or shoots. The bacteria enters the tree through a wound.

Trunks and branches

ANTHRACNOSE

This fungal disease affects currants and raspberries as well as trees. The bark splits and white patches with purple-tinged edges appear. The canes and branches eventually dry up. Precise symptoms vary slightly with the host plant and the particular fungus involved.

BARK BEETLES

The larvae of the bark (or engraver) beetles (insect family *Scolytidae*) bore into several species of fruit tree and can be extremely destructive. Their presence is indicated by a series of tunnels beneath the bark, running in all directions from a central point. These tunnels are formed by the newly hatched larvae as they bore away from the egg chamber.

CANE BLIGHT

Symptoms Fruit canes turn brown at the base and the extremities wither. The entire cane is soon affected by the disease and becomes brittle, making it easy to snap. This blight is caused by a fungus, *Leptosphaeria coniothyrium*, which usually enters the cane through frost cracks. It can also contaminate surrounding soil.

■ **Plant affected** Raspberry, particularly 'Norfolk Giant' and 'Lloyd George'.

■ **Treatment** Depending on the seriousness of the attack, one or several sprayings with a copper-based fungicide may eliminate the disease. However, it can be more effective to cut back the infected cane to below ground level and burn it. Disinfect your pruning tools afterwards. Plant a resistant raspberry variety.

CANKER

Cracks form on the bark, which become gradually wider, sometimes forming raised edges. The diseased tissue from underneath appears and a whitish gum oozes from the cankers. The diseased branch, and sometimes the entire tree or bush, withers and dies.

CLEARWING MOTH

■ **Symptoms** Shoots become brittle and, when broken, reveal a hollow, black interior. This is because the pith has been eaten by the white caterpillar of the clearwing moth (*Synanthedon tipuliformis*). The adult moth looks rather like a wasp. The larvae burrow into the shoots and pupate the following year; exit holes can be seen on stems in early summer.

■ **Plants affected** Red, white and blackcurrant, apple.

■ **Treatment** There is no effective control as the caterpillars cannot be reached inside the stems. In winter, cut back the affected shoots to where the pith is no longer discoloured and burn them.

FIREBLIGHT

This serious disease affects apples, pears and quinces, causing the foliage and then the branches to dry up completely. It is highly infectious, and the bacteria that causes the disease is easily spread by rain splash or on pruning tools.

GUMMOSIS

■ **Symptoms** A sticky, viscous, yellowish brown gum oozes from a wound on the trunk or branches. Stem and leaf lesions may also develop but these are less common. The fungal disease may be caused and spread by a simple insect sting, and the affected trees and bushes gradually wither and die. The oozing gum is the tree's response to an attack. This disease is encouraged by cool, damp conditions.

■ **Trees affected** Apricot, cherry, peach, plum.
■ **Treatment** Avoid damaging the tree. Prune at the height of the growing season. Scrape off the gum and paint the wound with a product that protects the healing scar. Prune out infected growth to healthy wood. Spray with an approved copper-based fungicide and feed with liquid nettle manure to strengthen new growth.

LEOPARD MOTH

■ **Symptoms** The creamy yellow caterpillars of the leopard moth (*Zeuzera pyrina*) bore into the trunk or branches making a network of tunnels where they stay until they pupate. The branches become brittle and may easily snap on a windy day. Another sign of infestation are pellets of compacted sawdust, which are the caterpillar's excrement, coming from one of the entry or exit holes. The infestation often consists of only one caterpillar, but this can still be disastrous if present in the trunk of a young tree.
■ **Trees affected** Apple, birch, hawthorn, maple, oak, sorbus, sycamore.
■ **Treatment** Preventive measures are not possible as the attacks are sporadic. If caterpillars are found, prune and burn the infected branch. Alternatively, insert a piece of wire into the tunnels to skewer the caterpillar.

SHOT-HOLE BORER

■ **Symptoms** The branches and trunk are riddled with tiny holes, each marked by a pile of sawdust, surrounded by a reddish brown canker. The tree gradually withers and dies. This is caused by a small brownish black insect (*Xyleborus dispar*), whose larvae burrow into the tree to pupate. Attacks usually occur on trees that are growing under stressful conditions and should not be a problem on vigorous fruit trees.
■ **Trees affected** Cherry, sweet chestnut, apple, pear, plum.
■ **Treatment** Destroy the larvae by pushing wires into the tunnels or, more effectively, cut out and burn the infested branches. Insecticides are ineffective as the larvae are protected by the bark.

SPUR BLIGHT

● **Symptoms** Purplish blue patches appear around young shoots and buds. The blight then spreads down to the canes, which turn a silvery grey colour and are covered with prominent black spots. The canes will produce virtually no fruit the following spring. Caused by a fungus, *Didymella applanata*, this blight is active during hot, wet summers.
■ **Plants affected** Loganberry, raspberry.
■ **Treatment** Cut out and burn the heavily infected canes and spray with an approved copper-based fungicide at regular intervals from leaf bud burst to blossom time.

WOOLLY APHID

■ **Symptoms** The bark is split and swollen and a cottony, white 'wool' appears on the trunk and branches. The reddish brown aphids (*Eriosoma lanigerum*) are about 2mm long and are sometimes visible. The aphids first appear in spring and suck sap from cracks in the bark and from young shoots. Their ability to reproduce by parthenogenesis (without fertilisation) means that a single aphid can produce as many as 100 offspring, which hibernate inside crevices in the bark.
■ **Tree affected** Apple.
■ **Treatment** Encourage natural predators such as ladybirds, lacewings and birds, who feed on this aphid, into the garden. Use a forceful water jet to wash off the woolly cover, then spray with an approved treatment as soon as the aphids appear in spring.

Leaves

BLACKCURRANT RUST

■ **Symptoms** Yellow-ochre blisters appear on the underside of the leaves, which wither and fall, leaving bare branches. This is caused by fungus that hibernates on conifers in the form of orange blisters that burst and release its spores. These spores contaminate currant bushes causing more blisters, which in turn release spores that reinfect conifers and thereby perpetuate the cycle.
■ **Bushes affected** Red and blackcurrant.
■ **Treatment** Avoid planting conifers and currant bushes in close proximity. Treat with an approved copper-based fungicide. The disease is spread through rain splash and the spores need moisture to germinate and infect, so make plants less susceptible by preventing damp, warm conditions where a film of moisture can develop on the leaves.

BLACKFLY

This aphid's dark colour makes it easily visible against foliage. Colonies tend to collect at the ends of branches on a number of fruit trees, feeding on sap and distorting growth. Spray with a combined solution of derris and pyrethrins.

BUFF-TIP MOTH

Branches are quickly stripped as the leaves are systematically eaten by caterpillars of the buff-tip moth, with their distinctive black-and-yellow chequered markings.

CAPSID BUG

The leaves of affected trees and shrubs look as if they have been riddled with shot.

CORYNEUM BLIGHT

- **Symptoms** This fungal disease is characterised by the appearance of small patches – about 1mm across, purplish red in the centre and edged with brown – on the leaves. These patches die and leave numerous little holes, and the leaves eventually fall. The disease can also affect the shoots, causing cankers and gum ooze, as well as flower buds, which dry up and drop. Patches on the fruit have a grey or black centre, which sometimes becomes pitted, revealing the stone. This is caused by the *Coryneum beijerinckii* fungus.
- **Trees affected** Apricot, peach, almond, cherry, plum.
- **Treatment** Spray with a fungicide containing copper. Remove affected branches when pruning. Build up the trees vigour by spraying them with liquid nettle manure during summer and water well in dry weather.

CURRANT APHID

- **Symptoms** The leaves turn from green to yellow and then red. They become deformed and blistered, and eventually wither and die. The disease is caused by the yellow currant aphid (*Cryptomyzus ribis*), which becomes active as the buds open.
- **Bushes affected** Red and blackcurrant.
- **Treatment** Encourage natural predators or spray with derris or pyrethrins.

DOWNY MILDEW

This fungal disease widely affects vines and can completely destroy several vine stocks.

ERMINE MOTH

- **Symptoms** Tents of silken webs can be seen woven around clusters of leaves. These are made by the ermine moth to house its small yellowish caterpillars that feed on the juicy foliage.
- **Trees affected** Apple, apricot, peach, plum, quince.
- **Treatment** Hang sticky cardboard traps to catch adult moths. Prune and burn infested branches to kill caterpillars.

FIREBLIGHT

This serious disease affects apples, pears and quinces, causing the foliage and then the branches to dry up completely. Lift and burn affected trees.

GREENFLY

- **Symptoms** Although its colour allows this aphid to blend with the green of the foliage, the effects of its presence are unmistakable. Afflicted leaves become deformed, curl up, turn yellow and fall. However, there is usually time for the leaves to grow back, as greenfly generally attack in early spring.
- **Plants affected** Most fruit.
- **Treatment** Use predators, such as ladybird larvae, which are widely available by mail order. Keep these predators in your garden by building a ladybird shelter from hollow sticks or a bundle of thorny prunings to protect them during winter. If aphids become a problem, remove quickly by spraying with derris or pyrethins. Feed with liquid nettle manure to aid recovery.

HAWTHORN RUST

- **Symptoms** Orangey yellow patches appear on the surface of the leaves while the undersides are covered with lattice-like swellings. This variety of rust is caused by a fungus (*Gymnosporangium globosum*), which hibernates on junipers, developing kidney-shaped galls. Light brown gelatinous blisters then appear and release spores that contaminate nearby fruit trees. Swellings develop on the leaves of these trees and, when mature, release spores that reinfect junipers.
- **Trees affected** Apple, crab apple, juniper, pear, quince.
- **Treatment** Avoid planting pears, apples, crab apples and quinces near junipers. Spray with a fungicide containing copper.

MEALY PLUM APHID

■ **Symptoms** As the pale green mealy plum aphid (*Hyalopterus pruni*) bites into the leaves on which it feeds, it secretes a honeydew on which a fungus develops. This mould prevents the leaves from breathing, so they wither and die. Each aphid's body is covered in a waxy substance that gives it a 'mealy' appearance. Colonies of aphids are found on the underside of leaves or on shoot tips.

■ **Trees affected** Most fruits with stones.

■ **Treatment** From late spring, spray with a fatty acid, oil or derris-based product if the aphids build up.

PEACH LEAF CURL

■ **Symptoms** The leaves curl up and change from green to yellow and then to bright red or purple. These symptoms are accompanied by the appearance of characteristic blisters. The leaves drop and young shoots become deformed. Gum will ooze from the affected area. Peach leaf curl is caused by a fungus of the genus Taphrina. It develops in early spring when the weather is cold and wet after a mild winter.

■ **Trees affected** Almond, cherry, nectarine, peach.

■ **Treatment** Spray with a copper fungicide in late winter. As soon as the buds begin to swell in early spring, spray with Bordeaux mixture to prevent spores from entering the buds. Repeat two weeks later and again just before the leaves drop. Erect polythene covers over fan-trained trees to keep off rain.

PLANT SUCKERS

■ **Symptoms** The leaves curl upwards, becoming deformed and stunted before dropping. Affected buds do not develop. The symptoms are caused by a yellow sap-sucking insect that is about 4mm long. Its larvae appear in spring. The most common are the apple sucker (*Psylla mali)* and the pear sucker (*Psylla piricula*).

■ **Trees affected** Apple, fig, pear.

■ **Treatment** In early summer, when the pest becomes active, spray the tree with a fatty acid, oil or an approved, bifenthrin-based product to prevent damage to the plants.

PLUM POX

■ **Symptoms** The leaves become deformed and a light-coloured mottling appears along the veins. The fruit also becomes misshapen and covered with mottling, and sometimes oozes gum. This viral disease, also known as Sharka, is transmitted by an aphid, which may be accidentally introduced into your garden on new plum rootstocks.

■ **Trees affected** Peach, plum.

■ **Treatment** There is no known treatment for this serious disease. In Britain, suspected outbreaks must be reported immediately to DEFRA (the Department for the Environment, Food and Rural Affairs). It is best to destroy the crop to avoid spreading the virus.

POWDERY MILDEW

■ **Symptoms** The upper surface of the young leaves, shoots and flower trusses are covered with the characteristic white powdery mould of this fungal disease. The foliage becomes deformed, growth is stunted and diseased flowers do not set. Affected fruits may crack and split because they are unable to expand normally. They may also develop brown patches and the leaves fall.

■ **Trees affected** Apple, grape, gooseberry, melon, peach, quince, vine.

■ **Treatment** Remove and burn affected leaves and shoots. Spray infected plants with Bordeaux mixture at the first sign of the disease and repeat treatment several times, once a fortnight. Space plants well to prevent them being overcrowded and to avoid humid conditions.

RED SPIDER MITE

These tiny mites, easily recognised by their bright red colour, are found on most species of fruit tree in hot, dry weather. Affected leaves turn yellow and become covered with greyish mottling. The leaves eventually wither and fall.

SCALE INSECT

■ **Symptoms** A number of spots can be seen on the shoots and underside of the leaves. These are accompanied by an accumulation of waxy or cottony threads and large amounts of soot-like fungus (genus *Apiosporum*), which develop on the leaves of infested plants.

■ **Trees affected** Apple, fig, pear, plum, vine.

■ **Treatment** Spray the infested plants with an approved fatty acid or oil-based insecticide.

SILVER LEAF

Silvery grey patches appear on the leaves of a few branches and gradually spread to the rest of the foliage. The tree withers and dies. This fungal disease mainly attacks plums, but can also affect trees in the family *Rosaceae* (apples, cherries, plums and peaches).

WINTER MOTH

The winter moth caterpillar attacks soft fruit bushes as well as most types of fruit trees, especially cherries, plums, apples and pears.

Flowers

APPLE-BLOSSOM WEEVIL

■ **Symptoms** Flower buds fail to open, turn brown and wither. Inside are tiny white grubs. On raspberries, the peduncles (fruit stalks) are cut. The apple-blossom weevil (*Anthonomus pomorum*) has a brown and white shell with a characteristic 'V' on its back. It lays its eggs in the flower buds, which are then killed by the grubs.

■ **Trees affected** Apple, pear, raspberry.

■ **Treatment** Protect buds at risk by spraying with an approved insecticide at regular intervals as the young growth develops in spring and early summer.

FRUIT MOTH

■ **Symptoms** Flower buds are eaten and woven together with silken webs, which causes them to dry up and wither. The pest is a green, brown-headed caterpillar.

■ **Trees affected** Most fruit, including fig, lemon.

■ **Treatment** Treat infected trees with an insecticide containing pyrethrins or rotenone (derris).

MONILIA BLOSSOM BLIGHT

■ **Symptoms** The flowers bloom and then wither, closing together to form a fairly compact, brown mass. This wilt is caused by a fungus of the genus *Monilia*, which can cause extensive damage to trees if left untreated.

■ **Trees affected** All trees bearing fruit that contain pips or stones.

■ **Treatment** Remove and burn affected parts to prevent the blight from spreading. Spray with copper or sulphur as soon as the tree begins to flower. Fungicides containing mancozeb are effective if applied in autumn, and in spring at bud burst.

WINTER MOTH

The winter moth caterpillar attacks a number of plants and the flowers of fruit trees.

Fruit

ANTHRACNOSE

■ **Symptoms** This disease affects stored fruit. Blisters appear on skin lesions, caused by a fungus, *Glomerella cingulata*, which enters the fruit via the pores on lesions.

■ **Trees affected** Apple, pear, quince.

■ **Treatment** Don't store damaged or bruised fruit. At the first sign of anthracnose, remove and burn affected fruit to prevent the disease from spreading.

APPLE SAWFLY

■ **Symptoms** The skin of the fruit has a long scar running from the peduncle (fruit stalk), while insect excrement pellets fall from a round hole. Inside are foul-smelling tunnels containing caterpillars of the apple sawfly (*Hoplocampa testudinea*) as they bore through the skin of the fruit to feed on the flesh. The larvae hatch out of cocoons in the soil in spring and burrow into the young fruit, often causing them to drop early.

■ **Trees affected** Apple, plum.

■ **Treatment** Remove and burn any infested young fruit to prevent the caterpillars causing further damage. If the pest becomes a problem, spray with a bifenthrin or pyrethrin-based product.

BOTRYTIS

Also known as grey mould, this disease causes fruit to become covered with a whitish furry fungus, while the flesh becomes soft and then dries up. The fruit eventually rots.

BROWN ROT

■ **Symptoms** The fruit (on the tree or in storage) bears signs of rot in concentric circles with pale beige blisters. The rot gradually spreads and eventually affects the whole fruit. This rot is caused by a fungus of the genus *Monilia*, which is carried by rain, wind, birds and insects. The mycelium (a strand of fungal growth) enters the fruit via an insect bite or blemish.

■ **Trees affected** All trees whose fruit contains pips or stones.

■ **Treatment** Burn rotten fruit and do not put the dead leaves on the compost heap. Treat with an approved fungicide spray in the spring and repeat as directed.

CODLING MOTH

■ **Symptoms** The fruit ripens prematurely and falls from the branches. The flesh is riddled with tunnels made by the larvae of the codling moth (*Cydia pomonella*). The openings where the caterpillars enter the fruit are marked by small piles of dark brown, sawdust-like insect excrement pellets. The pale pink, brown-headed caterpillars bore into the centre of the fruit and feed on its flesh. When it is time to pupate, they leave the fruit and burrow under the bark.

■ **Trees affected** Apple, sweet chestnut, pear, walnut, peach, plum.

■ **Treatment** Hang pheromone traps in the branches to attract the moths and reduce attacks. The moths are attracted by the smell of the sticky boards, get too close and become stuck and die. Treat with an insecticide containing bifenthrin, spraying several times at three-weekly intervals.

FRUIT FLY

■ **Symptoms** The fruit contains tiny larvae that feed on the flesh and reduce it to pulp. The fruit rots whether it is being stored or is still on the tree. The larvae of several types of flies are responsible for the devastation after they emerge from eggs laid in the developing fruit.

■ **Trees affected** Most fruit.

■ **Treatment** If the problem becomes a nuisance, spray with products containing derris or pyrethrins.

GRAPE VINE MOTH

■ **Symptoms** Vines are attacked by two generations of reddish, black-headed caterpillars, about 1cm long, laid by the grape vine moth (*Eupoecillia ambiguella*). The first devours part of the flowers and uses the rest of them to form a silky nest. The second bores into the grapes, which turn purplish brown, wither and rot.

■ **Plant affected** Vine.

■ **Treatment** Spray with an organic insecticide containing pyrethrins or rotenone (derris).

HAZELNUT WEEVIL

■ **Symptoms** Each infected hazelnut is pierced by a small hole, 1–2mm across, and the shell is empty. This condition is caused by a weevil (*Balaninus nucum*), which lays an egg inside the developing fruit. The larva feeds on the flesh of the hazelnut as the shell hardens. It exits the fruit in order to pupate by boring through the shell and then dropping onto the ground.

■ **Tree affected** Hazelnut.

■ **Treatment** Insecticides are ineffective against this pest owing to the hard hazelnut shells. However, since the larvae pupate in the ground at a depth of only a few centimetres, rotavating or deep digging around the base of the affected tree tends to bury them deeper and destroy them.

PLUM POX

This serious disease is caused by the plum pox virus. It affects the fruits of stone fruit trees, such as peaches, apricots, nectarines and plums, which become misshapen and mottled, and sometimes ooze gum. It also affects the leaves. In Britain, you are obliged to report this disease to DEFRA (the Department for the Environment, Food and Rural Affairs) at the first sign of an outbreak. There is no known treatment.

POCKET PLUM

■ **Symptoms** The fruit does not develop but becomes wrinkled and elongated without swelling. It has no pulp or stone, but instead a hollow pocket, and becomes covered with a light, pinkish down. The fruit stays green, then drops prematurely. This disease is caused by a fungus (*Taphrina pruni*), which affects the developing fruit.

■ **Tree affected** Plum.

■ **Treatment** There is no successful treatment. Although this fungus overwinters in the twigs on the tree, it may not attack the tree every year. To minimise damage, remove any affected plums promptly, preferably before they become covered in down. Fortunately, it is unusual for the entire tree to be infected.

SCAB

■ **Symptoms** The fruit becomes cracked, allowing parasitic infestations to enter, and covered with dark brown scabs. In addition, the fruit is sometimes deformed, and the infected part is harder to the touch. The leaves can also be affected as well as the fruit. This disease is caused by a fungus of the genus *Venturia*.

■ **Trees affected** Apple, pear.

■ **Treatment** Treat with an approved fungicide based on copper or sulphur.

120 Fruit planner

USE THIS PLANNER TO SEE WHEN TO PRUNE, FEED AND TEND YOUR FRUIT TREES AND BUSHES IN ORDER TO GET A CONTINUOUS CROP OF FRUIT TO HARVEST THROUGHOUT THE YEAR. IF INSECTS AND BIRDS ARE NOT TO REAP THE BENEFITS OF YOUR EFFORTS AND TAKE PRECAUTIONS AT THE APPROPRIATE TIME.

	JANUARY	FEBRUARY	MARCH	
GENERAL	plant, feed, spray	plant, feed	plant, feed	
APPLES	prune	prune	begin pest control	
BLACKBERRIES	cut back new plants	plant		
CHERRIES			begin pest control	
CURRANTS Black	prune new plants	prune	prune, feed	
CURRANTS Red and white	prune new plants	prune	prune, feed	
FIGS			plant	
GOOSEBERRIES	prune new plants		prune, feed	
PEACHES AND NECTARINES	feed established fan-trained plants	prune new plants, spray against peach leaf curl	pollinate, spray	
PEARS	prune	prune	begin pest control	
PLUMS			prune large trees	
RASPBERRIES	cut back new plants	prune		
summer fruiting			plant, prune	
autumn-fruiting			prune	
STRAWBERRIES				
summer fruiting		bring under glass or cover to force	disbud new plants	
autumn-fruiting			plant, disbud, feed	
VINES (OUTDOOR)			prune	

	APRIL	MAY	JUNE	
	protect blossom from frost, mulch, water	protect blossom if needed, mulch, water	control pests, weed, harvest	GENERAL
	continue pest and disease control	limit crop on young trees, start biological control, prune	continue pest control	APPLES
		tie in new canes	tie in new canes, control pests and diseases	BLACKBERRIES
	control pests, prune	control pests, prune	harvest, prune	CHERRIES
				CURRANTS Black
				CURRANTS Red and white
	feed, prune		stop new shoots	FIGS
	spray against sawfly	thin, control pests and diseases	continue pest control, summer prune, harvest	GOOSEBERRIES
	protect fruitlets	thin, control pests and diseases, prune fans	shape, thin	PEACHES AND NECTARINES
	continue pest and disease control	limit crop on young trees, start biological control, prune	continue pest control	PEARS
	spray unles in blossom	begin pest control	thin fruits, prune	PLUMS
		control weeds		RASPBERRIES
			spray	summer-fruiting
				autumn-fruiting
			propagate	STRAWBERRIES
	feed forced plants	feed forced plants, control mould	protect from birds, harvest	summer-fruiting
	disbud, feed	disbud		autumn-fruiting
	treat against mildew	stop shoots, spray	stop shoots, spray	VINES (OUTDOOR)

	JULY	AUGUST	SEPTEMBER	
GENERAL	harvest, protect from birds and other pests	harvest, destroy fruit affected by rot	harvest, order new plants	
APPLES	water, continue pest control, thin fruit, prune espaliers and cordons	harvest, water, continue pest control, thin fruit, prune cordons/espaliers	harvest, store, prune cordons/espaliers	
BLACKBERRIES	tie in new canes	harvest	harvest, prune old canes, train new canes	
CHERRIES	harvest, prune	prune, spray	prune, spray	
CURRANTS Black	harvest	harvest		
CURRANTS Red and white	harvest	harvest		
FIGS	remove fruit formed this year, tie in	remove fruitlets so main fruit will form	harvest overwintered fruit	
GOOSEBERRIES	continue pest control, harvest	continue pest control, harvest		
PEACHES AND NECTARINES	protect fruit, prune	prune after picking	prune, protect	
PEARS	thin, prune cordons/ espaliers	harvest, prune cordons/ espaliers	harvest, store, prune cordons/espaliers	
PLUMS	prune	prune	harvest, prune	
RASPBERRIES summer-fruiting	control weeds, harvest	prune old canes	prune old canes	
RASPBERRIES autumn-fruiting	support canes	protect fruit from birds	harvest, protect	
STRAWBERRIES	propagate			
STRAWBERRIES summer-fruiting	harvest, cut back, feed	plant	plant	
STRAWBERRIES autumn-fruiting		harvest	protect fruits, harvest	
VINES (OUTDOOR)	stop shoots, spray	protect from birds	harvest	

OCTOBER	NOVEMBER	DECEMBER	
prepare new ground, remove diseased leaves and fruit	plant	plant, spray	**GENERAL**
harvest, store	harvest, plant, prune	prune, control pests and diseases	**APPLES**
prune old canes, tie in new canes	prune old canes, tie in new canes, plant		**BLACKBERRIES**
spray if necessary			**CHERRIES**
	take cuttings, prune, plant	take cuttings, prune	**CURRANTS** Black
	take cuttings, prune, plant	take cuttings, prune	**CURRANTS** Red and white
			FIGS
	take cuttings, prune, plant	take cuttings, prune	**GOOSEBERRIES**
	spray after leaf-fall		**PEACHES AND NECTARINES**
harvest, store	harvest, prune, plant	prune, control pests and diseases	**PEARS**
			PLUMS
	plant, prune		**RASPBERRIES** summer-fruiting
harvest, protect	plant		**RASPBERRIES** autumn-fruiting
plant	plant, tidy leaves		**STRAWBERRIES** summer-fruiting
spray			**STRAWBERRIES** autumn-fruiting
			VINES (OUTDOOR)

Resources and suppliers

Resources

Royal Horticultural Society
80 Vincent Square,
London SW1P 2PE.
Tel: 020 7834 4333
www.rhs.org.uk

National Vegetable Society
5 Whitelow Road, Heaton Moor,
Stockport SK4 4BY.
Tel: 0161 4427190
www.nvsuk.co.uk

Henry Doubleday Research Association
Ryton Organic Gardens, Coventry,
Warwickshire CV8 3LG.
Tel: 024 7630 3517
www.hdra.org.uk

National Society of Allotment and Leisure Gardeners
O'Dell House, Hunters Road,
Corby, Northants NN17 5JE.
Tel: 01536 266576
www.nsalg.org.uk

Allotments: a plot holder's guide
DCLG Publications, PO Box 236,
Wetherby, LS23 7NB
Tel: 0870 1226 236
email: communities@twoten.com
www.communities.gov.uk/index.asp?id=1503017

Royal Botanic Gardens, Kew
Kew, Richmond, Surrey TW9 3AB
Tel: 020 8332 5000
www.rbgkew.org.uk

Seed suppliers

DT Brown and Co
Bury Road, Kentford,
Newmmarket, Suffolk, CB8 7PR.
Tel: 0845 1662275
www.dtbrownseeds.co.uk

Samuel Dobie & Son
Long Road, Paignton,
Devon, TQ4 7SX
Tel: 0870 1123623
www.dobies.co.uk

Mr Fothergill's Seeds Ltd.
Gazeley Road, Kentford,
Newmarket, Suffolk, CB8 7QB.
Tel: 01638 751161
www.mr-fothergills.co.uk

S.E. Marshalls & Co.
Alconbury Hill, Huntingdon,
Cambs PE28 4HY.
Tel: 01480 443390
www.marshals-seeds.co.uk

Nickys Nursery Ltd
Fairfield Road, Broadstairs,
Kent CT10 2JU.
Tel: 01843600972
www.dtbrownseeds.co.uk

Organic Gardening Catalogue Riverdene Business Park, Molesey Road, Hersham,
Surrey KT12 4RG.
Tel: 0845 1301304
www.organiccatalog.com

The Real Seed Catalogue
Brithdir Mawr Farm,
Cligwyn Road, Newport,
Pembrokeshire, SA42 0QJ.
Tel: 01239 821107
www.realseeds.co.uk

Robinson's Mammoth Vegetable Seeds
Sunny Bank, Forton, nr Preston,
Lancs PR3 0BN.
Tel: 01524 791210
www.mammothonion.co.uk

Suttons Seeds
Woodview Road, Paignton,
Devon TQ4 7NG.
Tel: 0870 2202899
www.suttons-seeds.co.uk

Tamar Organics
Tavistock Woodlands Estate,
Gulworthy, Tavistock,
Devon PL19 8DE.
Tel: 01822 834887
www.tamarorganics.co.uk

Thompson & Morgan (UK) Ltd
Poplar Lane, Ipswich,
Suffolk IP8 3BU.
Tel: 01473 688821
www.thompson-morgan.co.uk

Edwin Tucker & Sons Ltd
Brewery Meadow, Stonepark,
Asburton, Newton Abbot,
Devon TQ13 7DG.
Tel: 01364 652233
www.edwintucker.com

Unwins Seeds
Alconbury Hill, Huntingdon,
Cambs PE28 4HY.
Tel: 01480 443395
www.unwinsdirect.co.uk

Index

Page references in **bold** indicate main entries.

A

B

C

D, E

Acknowledgments

Images from the Reader's Digest collection were previously published in *All Seasons Guide to Gardening* and *Secrets & Tips from Yesterday's Gardeners*. Abbreviations are used as follows: RD Reader's Digest; SC Sarah Cuttle; MW Mark Winwood; MT Maddie Thornhill.

Front cover t iStockphoto.com/Ursula Alter **b** iStockphoto.com/ Michael Westhoff **Spine front cover tl and back cover** iStockphoto.com/www.pmsicom.net 1 Gap Photos Ltd/Richard Bloom **2-3** iStockphoto.com/Tyler Stalman **4 t** iStockphoto.com/Fotosav **4 b** iStockphoto.com/Reinhold Tscherwitschke **6-7** Gap Photos Ltd/ S & O Mathews **9** iStockphoto.com/Franz Pfluegl **10** © RD/SC **11** iStockphoto.com/John Shepherd **12** The Garden Collection/ Georgina Steeds/ Liz Eddison **13, 16** © RD/SC **18** iStockphoto.com/ Knud Nielson **19** © RD/MW **21 tl, tr, cl, cr** © RD/MT **21 bl** iStockphoto.com/Astrida Valigorsky **21 br** Garden Picture Library/S Harte **22** © RD/SC **23** Mise au Point/N & P Mioulane **24 c** B Horizon/A. Schreiner **24 t** Rustica/G. Cotonnec **25** © RD/MT **26, 27, 28, 29, 30** © RD/MW **31** iStockphoto.com **32 l, c** © RD/SC **32 br** © RD/MW **33 tr** iStockphoto.com/Anne Kitzman **33 b** © RD/MW **34** © RD/MT **35** iStockphoto.com/Michel de Nijs **36** Mise au Point/A. Descat **37** iStockphoto.com/Audrey Pustovoy **38 tl** iStockphoto.com/ Roberto Adrian **38 tr, br** © RD/MW **39** iStockphoto.com/Flavia Bottazzini **40** iStockphoto.com/Monika Adamczyk **41** iStockphoto.com/ Robert Kyllo **42** iStockphoto.com/Rebekah Blocher **43** © RD/Mike Newton **44** © RD/MW **45** iStockphoto.com/Jim Jurica **46** © RD/SC **47 t** iStockphoto.com/Milos Luzanin **47 b** iStockphoto.com/Robert Kyllo **48** Mise au Point/A. Descat **49** iStockphoto.com/Marje Cannon **50** © RD/MW **51 t** iStockphoto.com/Greg Nicholas **51 b** iStockphoto.com/Svetlana Nicholas **52 l** iStockphoto.com/Richard Robinson **52 r** iStockphoto.com/Mario Hornik **53** © RD/MW **54 tl, tr** Mise au Point/N & P Mioulane **54 tc** Mise au Point/Noun & Gaellë **54 b** © RD/MW **55 t** iStockphoto.com/John Sigler **55 b** iStockphoto.com/David Rose **56 t** iStockphoto.com/Rafal Fabrykiewicz **56** © RD/MW **58** © RD/SC **59** © RD/MW **60** © RD/SC **61** © RD/MW **62** © RD/SC **63, 65** © RD/MW **76-77** Gap Photos Ltd/John Glover **78** Gap Photos Ltd/S & O Mathews **79** © RD/SC **80** iStockphoto.com/Judith Bicking **82** iStockphoto.com/Denis Sauvageau **83, 84, 85** © RD/MW **86 t** © RD/MT **86 b** © RD/MW **88** © RD/MW **89** iStockphoto.com/Dave Logan **89 bl, bc, br** © RD/MW **90** © RD/SC **91** iStockphoto.com/Stephanie Kuwasaki **92** iStockphoto.com/Katarzyna Grodzicka/ http://foto.hmmm.pl **93 t** iStockphoto.com/Isidor Stankov **93 b** iStockphoto.com/Bettina Anzeletti **94** © RD/MW **95** iStockphoto.com/SharAmbrosia Photography **96** iStockphoto.com/ George Green **98 l** iStockphoto.com/Angela Hill **98 r** iStockphoto.com **99 l** © RD/MT **99 c, r** © RD/MW **100 t** iStockphoto.com/Susana Morales **100 bl, bc, br** © RD/MW **101** iStockphoto.com/Czardases **102** iStockphoto.com/Ryan Miller **103** © RD/SC **104** iStockphoto.com/ Sandy Manter **105 l** iStockphoto.com/Hedda Gjerpen **105 r** iStockphoto.com/Asa Tordenmalm **107** iStockphoto.com/ Maurice van der Velden **108** iStockphoto.com/Andreas Steinbach **110** iStockphoto.com/David Pruter **111** Mise au Point/N & P Mioulane **112** iStockphoto.com/Alexander Kashlan **113** iStockphoto.com/ Garnham Photography.

Reader's Digest Fruit and Vegetable Gardening is based on material in *Reader's Digest Secrets and Tips from Yesterday's Gardens* and *All Seasons Guide to Gardening* published by The Reader's Digest Association Limited, London

The Reader's Digest Association Limited, 11 Westferry Circus, Canary Wharf, London E14 4HE **www.readersdigest.co.uk**

Editor Lisa Thomas
Art Editor Louise Turpin
Designer Keith Miller
Proofreader Barry Gage
Indexer Marie Lorimer

Reader's Digest General Books
Editorial Director Julian Browne
Art Director Nick Clark
Managing Editor Alastair Holmes
Head of Book Development Sarah Bloxham
Picture Resource Manager Sarah Stewart-Richardson
Pre-press Account Manager Sandra Fuller
Senior Production Controller Deborah Trott
Product Production Manager Claudette Bramble

Origination Colour Systems Limited, London
Printed and bound in China by CT Printing

We are committed to both the quality of our products and the service we provide to our customers. We value your comments, so please feel free to contact us on **08705 113366**, or via our website at **www.readersdigest.co.uk**

If you have any comments about the content of our books, email us at **gbeditorial@readersdigest.co.uk**

ISBN: 978 0 276 44205 6
BOOK CODE: 400-615 UP0000-1
ORACLE CODE: 250010675H.00.24

Fruit & Vegetable Gardening